D0366546

HEROIN
IS THE WORST
THING TO
EVER HAPPEN TO ME

A COLLECTION OF ESSAYS BY ALICIA COOK

Copyright © 2017 Alicia Cook
Cover Design © 2017 Creative Catalyst, LLC

Printed in the United States of America.
All rights reserved.

No part of this document may be reproduced or transmitted in any form, or by any means, without prior written permission of Alicia Cook.

This book is not intended to be a substitute for the medical advice of a licensed professional. The reader should consult with a professional on any matters relating to his/her health.

ISBN-13: 978-1540423269
ISBN-10: 1540423263

www.thealiciacook.com
www.creative-catalyst.net

Heroin is the Worst Thing to Ever Happen to Me contains stories of people who have experienced addiction. These are very personal accounts, written to shed light on this deadly epidemic and its nondiscriminatory nature. Due to the sensitivity of the topic, names may have been changed.

FOREWORD

Written By: Steve Rogers
Executive Producer
PBS – Driving Jersey, Here's The Story

Like my mother and father before me, I grew up in New Jersey, the youngest of four children. We lived a thoroughly "Jersey" life. My folks grew up in the same town, met at a wedding through mutual friendships, got married themselves, and spent their early years together in those familiar North Jersey neighborhoods, overlooking the Hudson River and the City beyond.

We summered at the Shore and eventually moved there permanently--a very Jersey migration path. I promptly escaped after college and moved to New York, again, another typical migratory journey, albeit one for the younger tramps that were told they were *Born to Run.*

After living in the City for ten years, and now a father, I moved back to New Jersey. As I readjusted to the atmosphere, I realized I finally felt at home in my home state. All the things I forgot, I relearned with enthusiasm. All the people and places I used to know, I revisited with a deeper appreciation. And all the stuff that had always been a mystery to me, I sought out, which, in part, led to the creation of my documentary series.

I say *in part* because the other interest in exploration had nothing to do with New Jersey, and everything to do with a gnawing interest in people, a curiosity in the clockwork of human beings; what makes us who we are, what we do, how we do, *why* we do.

When things affect my "neighbors" or myself, I go in search of the reasons. Throughout the run of my documentary series, I have explored a number of stories and situations that are one or the other or, in some cases, both.

In the midst of the Great Recession, we judged the distance between the American Dream and the American reality. We have investigated how NGOs and art groups are working together to improve urban environments, short term and long term. And, after Hurricane Sandy devastated the Northeast, we reflected how people were affected and captured the extraordinary efforts of ordinary folks helping put lives back together.

As the accounts of the Heroin Epidemic, as it has become known, became a regular news story and part of our daily conversation, and yet, truly not part of my life experience, I decided to explore it, to understand it, or at least to be less ignorant about it.

The statistics and *then-and-now* comparisons are readily available and, usually, lead or close most news stories. There are always pictures or videos of needles piercing veins, a lot of finger pointing, and headlines about the most recent big bust and how it's going to "Make a difference."

Despite all of these news stories, people keep dying in the towns where I grew up, families continue to mourn, and neighbors continue to whisper.

For the episode, I sought out a fellow explorer, one who's been on the path longer than me, someone who connects to the issue because she's been affected by it, and looks long and hard at it because of a deep need to know...not for work, not for a news story, but because it's under her skin. Those are the best people for connecting the dots.

Alicia Cook is an authority, albeit a reluctant one, because she lost her cousin, Jessica Cook, to a heroin overdose in 2006, and she is haunted. Indeed, she welcomes spirits who have passed, as if she is their spokesperson, as if she can't shake it, as if it is her purpose, and so it is.

"I have someone else for us to talk to," she often told me as we collected interviews with fellow travelers on this road. She'd go deeply into their story, fulfilling the arch with a sense of drama and heartbreak in her voice, as if she was living or re-living it herself.

The process took longer than I imagined, six months of filming. It could have taken six years, and we still wouldn't have had all the answers we sought from the start. She mined and explored people like herself, the loved ones in the ripple of abuse and loss, those confused in the wake, but with an urgent need to tell their story, both for therapeutic reasons and also as a wake-up call.

We intentionally did not interview any active users. There were no shots of needles and veins. We spoke to some who were in recovery.

"I want this to be a film about those affected by those who use," Alicia told me, "because this is a *family disease*, because that side of the story is rarely ever told in a comprehensive way, and *we* need to heal, and we do so best when we can share and help others. We also happen to have first-hand knowledge of what our loved one was like before and after." Before and after. *Before and after.*

At our last shoot, at an opening along the Navesink River at sunset, a tremendous flock of birds flew in a crazy, excited wave above us. Hundreds of little black angels dotted the sky. The sound they made, which can only be compared to the sound of children laughing as they run, made us laugh along with them. It was one of the few, truly bright moments of our entire six-month journey together.

"Did you plan this?" Alicia asked with a smile. It was well deserved; proof maybe that she was going in the right direction, with the right people, for the right reasons.

We were there to do a final interview, a wrap-up of all we had learned, what she had illuminated for the audience. It was really the only question I had left for her, although, truth-be-told, despite our long production schedule and the many interviews we did together, I was still left with many *whys* and *what-fors*. I asked her for her conclusions. She took some time to consider.

"I've come to term with the fact," she said, "that I'll never come to terms with the facts."

Instead, she suggested that what she did find along the way and continues to, is hopefulness, because ultimately, like life, it's about confusion and hope. We never completely understand it, but we have no choice but to expect that there is always tomorrow and we take comfort and inspiration from others who share the same mixed emotions.

We can learn. We can influence others, especially our own family members, with an unguarded display of love and tears. Watching and listening to Alicia share tales of this journey with all of the people she met and introduced us to, I realized that the best any of these folks can do for each other, and others equally affected, is talk about it and map the terrain.

Maybe we learn a little bit more, and we help someone else who's on the road just behind us.

"I might not make it out of this alive.
I wish I never tried it."

Jessica Cook
1987 - 2006

INTRODUCTION

In 2015, 52,000 people in the United States overdosed on drugs and died. Never in recorded history had narcotics killed so many Americans in a single year. According to New York Magazine, the drug-induced death toll was so staggering, it helped reduce life expectancy in the United States for the first time since 1993.[1]

This book will not stop the heroin epidemic. As I write, as you read, in the days that follow, the heroin epidemic will not slow down just because I wrote this and you read it; that is not my intention with this book.

What I do hope this book does, is comfort the collateral damage of the disease of addiction: the families and the loved ones.

The ones who, with clear eyes, watch their child, husband or wife, sibling, cousin, niece or nephew, aunt or uncle, friend, neighbor, or co-worker slip away.

In the following pages, you will hear from people who have "been there." Everyday warriors who fight tirelessly and endlessly to create change, in hopes another is saved from the same fate.

Though some names have been changed, these pages contain real accounts from real people who battle addiction or love someone who struggles with addiction.

---

[1] http://nymag.com/daily/intelligencer/2016/12/the-opioid-epidemic-is-a-symptom-of-toxic-greed.html

I hope that after reading, those enduring this utter nightmare feel a little less isolated, stigmatized, and helpless. I hope you find courage. I hope your inner fire gets reignited; because families run down by addiction have two options:

surrender or fight back.

I hope everyone going through this chooses the latter.

Families, you are not alone – you are, unfortunately, one of many -- and each and every voice in this battle to combat the worst heroin epidemic in the last 20 years, matters. If you put your hand over your chest and still feel your heart beating – you're alive, and you can make a difference.

I would like to dedicate this collection of work to my cousin, Jessica Cook, who couldn't be here today, but is the reason why I stand here today.

Thank you.

"We're the ones left behind
who have to get up every day
and realize what happened;
and that's hard, that's very hard."

Robert Cook
Here's the Story: A Family Disease

Originally Published on the Huffington Post on January 8, 2016

LESSONS LEARNED

Heroin is the worst thing that has ever happened to me.

Heroin is holding the person I used to be hostage. I used to laugh more. I used to be more light-hearted and whimsical. I used to smile in more than just pictures.

I try to remember the moment my world began to revolve around it.

It is mentioned in nearly every conversation I have, even when it's not said outright, but in knowing glances, exasperated sighs or pity stares.

Most of my hobbies have fallen by the wayside ever since heroin entered my life.

I used to write about more than this.
I used to read about more than this.

I am a phony. My normalcy is a charade. Heroin forces me to keep secrets from the people who matter most in my life. I can't tell my family how much pain I'm in because I can imagine the pain they are feeling too, and I don't want to add to it.

Like all families whose path it crosses, heroin has ruined some of the best parts of mine. We have fought with one another out of desperation, out of anger. We have said things we cannot take back.

Heroin is the un-welcomed guest who has ruined holidays, birthdays and weddings. Heroin is the elephant in every room I inhabit. If I am there, so is heroin. It's ever present.

Heroin has taken sleep away from me. The days of a peaceful night's slumber are far behind me. Heroin haunts me even when my eyes are closed. I go to sleep thinking about it; I wake up thinking about it.

My daily routine:

I wake up and think about heroin.
I go to work and think about heroin.
I talk on the phone and bring up heroin.

When it's really bad, I spend some days sick to my stomach, with very little strength and lacking the motivation to even get out of bed.

Heroin has aged me. I look in the mirror, and I know I look tired, gaunt and disheveled.

Heroin took my peace of mind and replaced it with a constant state of worry. I lost my innocence a long time ago — I admit, I miss the blissful ignorance that came with knowing nothing about this drug.

The deeper I fall into this world, the more scared I become. I know this drug kills people, but I can't stop its pull. It's out of my hands.

Heroin has taken so much from me over the years. Time I can never get back. People I will never see again. Memories I never had a chance to make.

And the craziest part of all of this? **I never touched the stuff myself.**

I have never used heroin, but I love someone who did. Addiction has such a large ripple effect, the collateral damage is immense, and what is hit the most and the hardest by heroin's shrapnel is the family, the loved ones.

Addiction is a "family disease." This nightmare became my reality, I never asked for this, and that is what gets me so angry at times. I woke up, and my entire life changed. It may never be the same. The thing is, even though I am not addicted to drugs, I am suffering just as much, though in a different way because the family witnesses helplessly how one lapse in judgment, one wrong decision, one chemical dependency, can ruin everything.

Yes, heroin has taken so much from me — but it hasn't taken away my voice. It will not take away my voice.

It is my hope to use my words to raise awareness about drug addiction and its direct effect on not only the user, but the user's family.

I started sharing my experiences, not to find answers, but to find momentary peace of mind. It was scary at first — but I am of the belief that one person's story may change someone else's and give a struggling individual or family member the strength to persevere through hard times.

I believe it was Bob Marley who said, "You never know how strong you are until being strong is your only choice."

And you never know who needs to hear exactly what you are saying. So families, stay strong. Never give up hope.

Originally Published in the Daily Advertiser on October 22, 2015

LESSONS LEARNED 2

I am not an addict.

But try and love one, and then see if you can look me square in the eyes and tell me you didn't become addicted to trying to fix them.

If you're lucky, they recover. If you're really lucky, you recover, too.

Loving someone addicted to drugs can and will consume your every thought. Watching their physical deterioration and emotional detachment to everything will make you the most tired insomniac alive.

You will stand in the doorway of their bedroom and plead with them that you *just want them back*. If you watch the person you love disappear right in front of your eyes long enough, you will start to dissolve too.

Those not directly affected won't be able to understand why you are so focused on their well-being, especially since, during the times of your loved one's active addiction, they won't seem so concerned with their own.

Don't become angry with these people. They do not understand. They are lucky not to understand. You'll catch yourself wishing that you didn't understand, either.

What if you had to wake up every day and wonder if today was the day someone you love was going to die? will become a popular, not-so-rhetorical question.

Drug addiction has the largest ripple effect I have ever witnessed firsthand.

It causes parents to outlive their children. It causes jail time and homelessness. It causes sisters to mourn their siblings. It causes nieces to never meet their aunts. It causes an absence before the exit.

An absence before the exit.

You will see your loved one walking and talking, but the truth is, you will lose them long before they actually succumb to their demons; which, if they don't find recovery, is inevitable.

Drug addiction causes families to come to fear a ringing phone or a knock on the door. It causes vague obituaries. I read the papers and I follow the news; it is scary. *Died suddenly* has officially become obituary-speak for *another young person found dead from a drug overdose.*

Drug addiction causes bedrooms and social media sites to become memorials. It causes the *yesterdays* to outnumber the *tomorrows*. It causes things to break; like the law, trust, and homes.

Drug addiction causes statistics to rise and knees to fall, as praying seems like the only thing left to do sometimes.

People have a way of pigeonholing those who suffer from addiction. They call them *trash, junkies,* or *criminals.* Addiction is an illness.[2] People addicted to drugs have families and aspirations.

You will learn that drug addiction doesn't discriminate. It doesn't care if the user came from a loving home or a broken family.

Drug addiction doesn't care if you are religious. Drug addiction doesn't care if you are a straight-A student or a drop-out. Drug addiction doesn't care to know your ethnicity. Drug addiction will show you that one decision and one lapse in judgment can alter the course of an entire life.

Drug addiction doesn't care. Period. *But you care.*

You will learn to hate the drug but love the addict. You will begin to accept that you need to separate who the person once was with who they are now.

It is not the person who uses, but the addict. It is not the person who steals to support their habit, but the addict. It is not the person who spews obscenities at their family, but the addict. It is not the person who lies, but the addict.

And yet, sadly... it is not the addict who dies, *but the person.*

---

[2]https://www.drugabuse.gov/publications/research-reports/comorbidity-addiction-other-mental-illnesses/drug-addiction-mental-illness

Originally Published in the Daily Advertiser on March 23, 2016

LESSONS LEARNED 3

In the previous story, I wrote, "Drug addiction causes an absence before the exit. You will see your loved one walking and talking, but the truth is, you will lose them far before they actually succumb to their demons; which, if they don't find recovery, is inevitable."

As loved ones of those who suffer from addiction, you may begin to grieve while they are still alive. I know I did. Addiction took a person I had known my entire life and turned her into someone who, at times, I didn't know at all. I found myself not only missing who the person was before addiction, but also mourning that person.

There are seven stages of grief. These stages are usually understood to be shock or disbelief, denial, bargaining, guilt, anger, depression, and acceptance and hope.[3]

Everyone, even members of the same family, goes through each stage differently since symptoms of grief can be emotional, physical, social or religious.

This is my experience. Drug addiction has proven to me, time and time again, that you can mourn the living.

---

[3] http://www.medicinenet.com/loss_grief_and_bereavement/article.htm

DISCLAIMER: Some of you may not agree with this article at all. I am not a medical professional or psychiatrist. I am just someone who has lost a loved one to addiction. It is important to interpret the stages loosely, and expect variations, but I felt it was important to share what I went through before my loved one even lost her life.

1. SHOCK and DISBELIEF

When addiction is first discovered, one may react to learning of this with numbed disbelief. I know I didn't feel anything the first few moments following the discovery that my loved one was addicted to drugs. My hands were shaking uncontrollably, and I was totally unaware. Though I didn't know how to process my feelings at the time, I knew my family's life was going to be changed forever, even if she survived. I learned that receiving life-altering news will evoke bodily reactions you can't control, like fainting and vomiting. Your body will try to save itself. Shock provides emotional protection from being overwhelmed all at once.

2. DENIAL

You may deny the severity of the situation, even if proof - like paraphernalia, failed drug tests and sunken, pinhole eyes - is staring you right in the face.

"She only used once," or "We can fix her and go about our normal lives again," or "She still looks like herself when she is sleeping," are phrases I heard myself saying. I wanted to believe heroin addiction was easily combated, even though the statistics said otherwise. In the typical seven stages of grief, this stage has been documented to last for weeks, but when it comes to addiction, you must react immediately. Every second counts once you learn your loved one is battling addiction.

3. ANGER

I read that anger is not a universal emotion during the grief process.[4] Yet, when it comes to losing who the person was before addiction took hold, anger is most definitely experienced by loved ones. I was mad, a lot. A LOT. Some days I was angry with her, other days I was angry at myself for not figuring it out sooner. I was mad at the proverbial clock for ticking before I could catch up. I was angry with people who started to treat us differently. I was angry at the news for taking so long to cover the heroin epidemic. I was angry with her "using buddies." I was angry with her "friends" who knew but didn't tell us, who urinated for her so she would pass drug tests. I was angry at people for not understanding.

Resources like Al-Anon or Nar-Anon can help families who know or have a feeling of desperation concerning the addiction of someone they care about.[5] These groups connect you to professionals and others who understand your problem as few others could.

4. BARGAINING

In a desperate attempt to get your loved one back before it is too late, you will bargain with the drug user.

Boy, will you bargain.

---

[4] http://www.stages-of-grief-recovery.com/7-stages-of-grief.html

[5] https://www.addiction.com/13881/go-al-anon-nar-anon/

I know families who have spent their savings or have taken second mortgages out on their home trying to rehabilitate their loved one. I know parents who have offered every incentive under the sun to their loved for each month they stayed clean.

Even if bargaining seems successful, it is nothing but a Band-Aid. It cannot and will not keep your loved one in recovery – only they can do that. If you are religious, you will even bargain with your higher power. Mine happened to be God. I cannot tell you how many prayers I said in hopes to be able to turn back the clock and do some things differently. I have lit countless candles in church with her name attached.

5. GUILT

As your loved one falls more and more into the world of addiction, they will become less and less recognizable to you. Watching someone destroy their lives – their precious lives – can infuriate and upset any bystander.

You may say things out of anger and frustration that you will later regret, should something happen to them. Hurtful words may leave your lips. You may have feelings of guilt over things you did or didn't do with your loved one leading up to and following the discovery of their addiction. Every single situation is different, but all I can say is, I learned that saying hurtful things will not make your loved one *snap out of it.*

Addiction is an illness that forever alters the way the brain operates – they will not react the way you might would.[6] I've seen parents crying in front of their child, only to have their child roll their eyes and walk the other way. This is not the child they raised – this is someone who is sick with addiction who still shares their likeness. Another thing I want to note here is at the end of the day, you will need to be able to sleep at night, and you don't want to make choices that will keep you up the rest of your life.

6. DEPRESSION

When you watch your loved one slip deeper and deeper into addiction, you may very well slip into depression. I know I felt so helpless.

I learned quickly there was nothing I could do other than be supportive, educate myself, not enable, and offer my assistance should they want it.

If they don't find recovery, this helplessness will mutate into a profound sadness. I had days I couldn't make it out of bed or focus on my daily tasks at work.

At the root of all of this is the fact that the only person who can save the person abusing drugs is that person. The willpower and drive have to come from within, whether they are a minor or not.

---

[6]https://www.drugabuse.gov/publications/drugs-brains-behavior-science-addiction/drugs-brain

7. ACCEPTANCE & HOPE

Whether they enter rehab, successfully find recovery, or continue using, you will eventually come to accept this as your "new normal." Although things will never be the same again, there is hope that life will go on.

Even when my loved one was still alive, but sick, I found myself becoming more functional. It was as if a fog had been lifted and my mind started working again. I knew I had to rebuild myself. I knew that whether they survived this or not, I had to survive.

At first, I felt guilty and a bit selfish for doing this – but self-preservation is essential. You only get one life as well. You will once again anticipate some good times to come, and yes, even find yourself laughing at jokes and smiling again.

It took years for my aunt and uncle to put a Christmas tree back up, but they did. It took me a very long time to even eat the meal my cousin and I would always split.

It is important to know that baby steps are still steps.

We all know how my story ended: *I lost my cousin.*

I lost my cousin to drugs almost two years before she actually died. But I know there are people out there still battling this "family disease." I want you to know that this is not a framework for what you will go through, as I am aware every situation is vastly different. I just wanted to share my experiences, because you are not alone. Unfortunately, you are in the company of many.

Originally Published in the Daily Advertiser on December 8, 2015

LESSONS LEARNED 4

The other night, someone yelled at me.

For someone who writes about addiction, you are judgmental!

I was many things that night: Mad. Hurt. Sad. Confused. Frustrated. At a loss - but judgmental? No. *No way.*

I wish I wasn't gaining notoriety for having one of the "best handles" on this subject. No one ever says to themselves, while reading articles like mine, *I wish I could relate to this.*

I wish I wasn't a part of this community, but I am. I know all too well what it's like to love a person who suffers from addiction.

I know what it's like to worry yourself sick. To cry yourself to sleep.

I know to watch out for pinhole pupils and subtle changes in behavior. To listen to them talk, make excuses and pile on lie after lie. I know what it's like to pretend to believe them because you are just too mentally exhausted for an argument at that given time.

I know what it's like to be confused all the damn time; to see their potential, to know what they are throwing away. I know what it's like to want their recovery more than they do. To be the one doing research on rehabs and other outlets for recovery.

I know what it's like to miss someone who is still standing right in front of you.

I know what it's like to wonder if each unexpected phone call is *the* phone call. I know what it's like to be hurt so badly and made so sick, a part of you wishes you would just get *the* phone call if nothing is going to change. You want that finality. You need the cycle to end. I know what it's like to hate yourself for even allowing yourself to find relief in that horrible thought.

I know what it's like to get the worst news of your life, and still walk into the grocery store, run your errands and smile at the cashier.

I know what it's like to become a part-time detective. You know you are going to find something, and you look until you do, so that you feel less crazy. So you can say to yourself, *I am not paranoid. This is happening again.*

I know what it's like to have your mind clouded; to turn into a functioning zombie. I know what it's like to be physically present at board meetings and dinner dates, but mentally gone.

I know what it's like to be really mad. Like, REALLY pissed off. Between the sadness, there is a lot of anger. I know what it's like to feel guilty for being so mad. Even knowing all you know about addiction, you are allowed to be angry. This is not the life for which you signed up.

I know what it's like to scour a bookshelf and not find what you are looking for because this illness is still so hard to talk about, let alone write about.

I know what it's like to hear someone argue that addiction is not an illness, but a "choice" or "social disorder." I know all too well that feeling of heat rising in your face as they go on and on about something they know nothing about.

I know what it's like to stop being angry with these people. As I mentioned once before, they do not understand. They are lucky not to understand. I know what it is like to catch yourself wishing that you didn't understand either.

I know the difference between enabling and empowering. I know there is a fine line between the two, and the difference can mean life or death. I know what it's like to the feel the weight of each day on your shoulders trying to balance the two.

I know what it's like to have "good days" and "bad days" but never "normal days." I have been through enough to know that things do not just change for the worse overnight; they can change in a millisecond. In a blink of an eye. As quickly as it takes two people to make a $4 exchange.

I know what it's like to feel stigmatized. To be the "cousin of a drug addict," a "friend of a drug addict," a "sibling of a drug addict," a "parent of a drug addict," a "neighbor of a drug addict." I know what it feels like to be handled with kid gloves because no one outside your toxic bubble knows what to say to help.

I don't know what the future holds for anyone who loves a substance abuser today. One thing I know for sure is I am not alone.

I write on addiction for a lot of reasons. I write to let loved ones know they are not alone. I write on addiction because, for far too long, many have felt isolated, hopeless and stigmatized by this illness.

Today I am writing on addiction to tell you that you are allowed to feel angry without feeling guilty. You are allowed to feel sad, mad or frustrated without feeling guilty. You are allowed to take a step back if you need a breather without feeling guilty.

With so many variables being out of your power, the one thing you are in control of is your own well-being. Feeling any of this at any point does not mean you are suddenly a judgmental person who does not understand addiction.

All of this does not mean you do not love this person unconditionally.

Alicia Cook presented this speech at Morris Knolls High School in New Jersey on May 13, 2016. It was then published on the Huffington Post on May 22, 2016.

LESSONS LEARNED 5

Heroin sucks. It really, really does. It sucks not just in the "man, that sucks" way but also in the literal way. It sucks the happiness out of homes. It sucks the trust out of relationships. It sucks the dreams from a peaceful night's sleep. It sucks the literal life out of those who use and those who watch those who use.

People still roll their eyes when I call addiction a disease. Yet, when I call it a FAMILY disease, I am not met with the same adversity. Something in the person breaks and they recognize, even but for a moment, that I am sick, physically and mentally ill, over what I watch unfold every day.

Maybe they can see it in my eyes. My very tired, dry, bloodshot eyes. Maybe they can feel it in my frail shoulder blades when they hug me and have no idea what to say other than "have you eaten today?" Maybe they can understand it when they hear me crying in the middle of the night even though I turned the shower and the sink on to kill the noise of my pain.

Yes, MY pain.

All because of a bag of powder that skulked into my life through the bloodstream of someone I love more than I can ever explain on paper.

I am never in denial. I know this drug. I know the statistics. I know the situation is dire. I know overdoses are killing more of us annually than automobile accidents. I know that one bag costs less than a meal at McDonald's. I know what Fentanyl[7], Suboxone[8], Vivitrol[9], and Narcan[10] are. I know why dealers stamp their wax folds.[11] I know the third day of withdrawal is the worst.[12] I know it costs $250 for a 45-minute session with a specialist who will just tell me everything I already know.

They need to want to save themselves.

I don't need to be addicted myself to know that it is poison. Each bag, a bullet. Each snort or injection, the spin of the cylinder. This is our generation's Russian Roulette.

I am sad a lot of the time. A home where addiction is present is oftentimes a painful place to live. It is hard to watch someone you care about spiral out of control and become someone you have to squint at to recognize. Memories will flood your mind, as you scramble to latch on to one - *just one* - happy reminiscence. It is difficult to see so clearly what their disease makes them so blind to their own potential, their own worth, and their own mortality.

---

[7] https://www.drugabuse.gov/drugs-abuse/fentanyl

[8] http://www.suboxone.com/treatment/suboxone-film

[9] https://www.vivitrol.com/

[10] https://www.narcan.com/

[11] http://www.nytimes.com/2006/08/01/nyregion/01INK.html

[12] http://americanaddictioncenters.org/withdrawal-timelines-treatments/heroin/

I am angry a lot of the time. I used to feel guilty saying that. I've learned it's okay for me to say, even out loud, "I am the collateral damage in this. I didn't ask for this." I used to walk on eggshells and talk and act very deliberately. I was afraid that something I would say would push them to use, or even worse, give up on themselves.

You're dope sick? Well, I'm heart sick.

I am happy a lot of the time. Which is a really odd thing for me to say, right? Since I am also sad, angry, helpless, and confused most of the time too. If I learned anything from this, it is families are resilient. *I am resilient.* After a sleepless night of praying the phone won't ring, or praying it will, the sun will rise and another day of my life will begin. Dishes need to be washed, laundry needs to get done, birthdays need to be celebrated. Yes, some days I am mailing it in - the fears that come along with addiction are all consuming - but some days I do smile and mean it.

I have good days, and bad days, but never normal days.

To anyone going through this with a loved one: I want you to know happy times can and will come again once you accept that you cannot "fix" your loved one. You simply (it's never simple) can't, but being *helpless* doesn't mean you *help less.* You can love them. You can support them. You can do everything in your power...everything but save them. I know as soon as I accepted this, I was able to let bits of joy enter my life again. This light didn't kill the darkness, but it brought with it moments of happiness and laughter nonetheless.

I beg you never abuse opioids like heroin, because that will be the first day of the end of your life. It is not a matter of *if* it will kill you, but *when.*

You are stronger than a lot of things, I am sure, but you are not stronger than this drug.

I pray that someone you love never tries it, for that is a pain I would not wish on my worst enemy.

I used to hear "You can't let it get to you like this," or "Just cut them out." *Just cut them out* - as if they were nothing more than a one-dimensional character on a poorly written crime drama. I am met with sympathy now, but more so, sadly, I am met with complete and utter understanding from people who can directly identify with my situation. As more and more families are affected by addiction, I hear less and less from the peanut galleries in both my real life and the comment sections of my articles. Perhaps they are too busy still thinking it could never happen to them. Or, more realistically, they are terrified it can.

Alicia Cook presented this speech at Mendham Township Middle School in New Jersey to 7th and 8th graders and their parents on December 6, 2016.

LESSONS LEARNED 6

Six weeks before my cousin Jessica died, we sat together in my living room. I was wearing a bathrobe, and she was wearing a long-sleeved black hoodie.

Long sleeves in July.

One of the last things she ever said to me that day was, "It is so much stronger than me. I wish I never tried it."

In my line a work, I speak with a lot families where addiction is present – and toward the end or at the end, every single person battling addiction has uttered that at least once.

I wish I never tried it.

Jess and I had a lot in common. She was a great student, more involved in extracurricular activities than I ever was. She came from a loving home and had everything she could ever want. She vacationed with her family and had her pick of colleges. She laughed a lot and made a lot of people laugh in return. She was outgoing and adventurous.

The only reason I stand here today and she does not, is because she decided to experiment with heroin, and I didn't.

That's THE ONLY REASON she isn't here.

She TRIED heroin. ONCE. Then, twice. And by then, she was already addicted. And ask any medical professional/addiction expert, and they will tell you – it is a hell of a lot easier to never try drugs than it is to ever get off of them, and stay clean. Especially when it comes to opiates.[13]

Public health officials have called the current opioid epidemic the worst drug crisis in American history, killing more than 33,000 people in 2015 alone. In 2015, for the first time, deaths from heroin alone surpassed gun homicides.[1415]

Parents – do not roll the dice. Talk to your children openly and honestly about drugs. If you see changes in behavior, confront them not as an accusatory measure, but as a preventative measure. You cannot protect your children from everything, especially this, but at least *right here and now*, you can take a proactive stance against the worst drug epidemic in our nation's history.

You can say "My kid would never use heroin." But this national health crisis stems from our youth experimenting with pills first, which is just synthesized heroin.[16] Pills soon dry up or become too expensive.[17] Heroin is just roughly $4 a

---

[13]www.alternet.org/drugs/37-quotes-heroin-users-addiction-and-struggle-stay-sober

[14]www.cdc.gov/mmwr/volumes/65/wr/mm655051e1.htm?s_cid=mm655051e1_w

[15]www.washingtonpost.com/news/wonk/wp/2016/12/08/heroin-deaths-surpass-gun-homicides-for-the-first-time-cdc-data-show/?utm_term=.950bf07d43a0

[16]www.opium.org/synthetic-opiates-list-drugs-derive-opium.html

[17]www.teens.drugabuse.gov/blog/post/connection-between-pain-medications-and-heroin

bag in many areas (cheaper than a six-pack of beer), making for a better, longer, and more affordable high.[18]

Do not say "Not my kid," because statistics state, beyond a shadow of a doubt, that the majority of active pill and heroin users right now fit your child's description, to a T.

Between 2006 and 2013, the number of first-time heroin users nearly doubled, and about 90% of these first-time users were white suburbanites, from good families, in their early twenties.[19]

Now is not the time to treat addiction like it is everyone's problem but yours, parents. Like you are above addiction. Like you parented better than the person living next door did. Addiction will creep into your home and your world in a blink of an eye.

Kids, never try an opiate – never think you can pop a pill or snort or shoot a line and remain in control, because you will not remain in control. You will destroy yourself and your family.

Do not bring addiction into your home, because, trust me, you do not want to be a part of this world, *my world*. It is dark, and cold, and sad, and life ruining.

If you are battling demons and emotions you cannot compute yourself, ask for help. Do not be ashamed. Self-medicating will not help.

---

[18] www.troyrecord.com/article/TR/20140526/ENTERTAINMENT/140529731

[19] www.washingtonpost.com/news/powerpost/wp/2016/03/23/the-color-of-heroin-addiction-why-war-then-treatment-now/?utm_term=.05be3caf7ad9

Originally Published in the Daily Advertiser on October 23, 2015

MEET TORI

According to a study conducted in 2013, an estimated 24.6 million Americans aged 12 or older had used an illicit drug in the past month. That's approximately one in every 10 Americans over the age of 12 – roughly equal to the entire population of Texas.[20]

Each has a unique story, and for far too long, many have felt isolated, hopeless and stigmatized by this illness. And I am not just talking about the user. Since 2010, the numbers have only risen, and for every one person battling Substance Use Disorder[21], there are numerous loved ones directly affected as well.

Drug addiction is a *family disease.* During any kind of active addiction, it is extremely rare only the user is affected.

Loving a someone who is battling addiction is both heartbreaking and exhausting. Addiction can and will destroy families as much as it destroys the user. Family members are torn between how to help and how to avoid enabling the addiction.

The reality of substance abusers is that the majority are just like everyone else. They have families, children, friends, lovers, spouses, co-workers and neighbors.

---

[20] https://www.drugabuse.gov/publications/drugfacts/nationwide-trends

[21] https://www.samhsa.gov/disorders

I spoke with Tori about her turbulent relationship with David, with whom she had fallen in love before his dark descent into the world of methamphetamine and opiates.

Tori did not wake up one day and say to herself, *I am going to fall in love with a drug addict,* or, *I am going to have a child with a drug addict.* Many loved ones aren't even aware of substance abusers' struggles until the lies they put into place in order to hide their habit begin to unravel.

When Tori discovered she was pregnant, the couple was happy and planned to raise their child together. However, a month into her pregnancy, David became withdrawn from her and his family.

Then, David left Tori. She was heartbroken and confused. Growing up in a sheltered home, she never even thought David's change in behavior had anything to do with drug abuse. She blamed herself for losing him.

David stayed in touch with Tori, regularly asking for updates on their baby as she progressed in her pregnancy. She invited him to her ultrasound appointment where she was going to discover the gender. Tori told me he seemed excited and agreed to go with her.

When the day of the appointment arrived, David was a no-show, and Tori was alone and heartbroken as the nurse announced she was having a baby girl.

She planned to name her baby Lily.

Communication with David in the months that followed was very sporadic, but Tori held out hope in getting her family back together before the baby's birth in June. She got her wish, but little did she know her dream come true would soon escalate into the biggest nightmare of her and her child's life.

Lily was born four days after her due date, and Tori described that day to me as the most "magical day" of her life. She was happy to be back together with David to share in the joys of parenthood.

What happened next, Tori never saw coming. The withdrawn, uncommunicative David returned. In hindsight, Tori realizes he had relapsed.

This time, he was angry. He began yelling and berating Tori at every opportunity. This quickly escalated into him beating Tori with his fists.

After one brutal fight, Tori recalled being thrown by David almost into their sleeping child's crib. David had no recollection of the abusive explosion and even asked Tori where the bruises all over her body came from.

Tori was terrified but didn't leave him. Like many victims of domestic abuse, her blame turned inward, and she believed herself to be the problem.[22] She was ashamed to admit she was getting beat on a regular basis.

---

[22] http://www.abuseandrelationships.org/Content/Survivors/victim_blaming.html

David's job conducted random drug testing of their employees. David failed for both methamphetamine and opiates and was let go from the company. This was the first valid piece of evidence that David was not only an abusive partner, but a drug abuser.

As soon as the drug test was positive, everything else over the last year began to fall into place and make sense. He had wrecked three cars. Some of Tori's possessions had gone missing. He could never hold down a job. He never slept. At the time, Tori was hopeful that since his problems were no longer hidden, he would seek help for his addiction.

Tori investigated rehab facilities and began to educate herself on addiction. Since addiction was never present in her family before, when David said he could beat this on his own, she believed him. She still didn't fully comprehend that addiction is not just a behavioral issue, but a chronic brain disorder.

He began working another job, and the abuse stopped. Tori believed this was a move in the right direction for her family.

Until the day she was doing laundry, and David's drug pipe fell out of his pocket.

After approaching him about it, he lashed out once again, violently. He was yelling, hitting, and ignoring her daily. David was working again, so most days, the abuse wouldn't occur until after the baby was asleep. A small, silver lining in Tori's bruised eyes.

Tori discovered a letter from David's employer stating he was terminated from his position. It was post-dated three weeks before Tori found the letter. Her world started spinning. David had been waking up and going to work every day the past three weeks...or so she had believed.

It is easy to pass judgment from the outside looking in, and Tori knows she should've left David a long time before she actually did. After she had found that letter, and he beat her for the last time, she found the courage within herself to call the cops.

He spent a few nights in prison. He appeared at Tori's doorstep weeks later, begging for money to support his habit. Tori described him at that moment as smelling of vinegar and sweat, with shallow cheeks and dirty clothes. She tried to convince him to get professional help one last time.

Tori didn't give him money and hasn't seen or heard from David since.

Thinking back, Tori knows the signs of addiction were obvious; but no one knows what it is like until they are in the throes of it. She admits to being in denial for most of their relationship. She admits to putting her own life and the life of her daughter at risk for far too long. She also recognizes her situation could have been much worse if she had never called the cops that day.

Tori did everything she could for David. She urged him relentlessly to seek professional help. She found him jobs. She encouraged him and loved him unconditionally. And it could have cost her everything.

"Many would take this experience and just play the victim card the rest of their lives. I refuse to be the victim," Tori stated, adamantly. "I let this terrible ordeal empower me. I am smarter because of this. I am stronger because of this."

Her bruises have healed. Her daughter has grown into a beautiful and healthy toddler.

"Lily is the greatest good David will ever create, and it kills me to think about how he could possibly never even know her," Tori said, speaking about her daughter.

The last thing I asked Tori was what she hopes people take away from her story.

"I hope others read my story, see they aren't alone, and maybe find the strength to get themselves out of bad situations," she explained. "I just think maybe letting you share my story will touch someone's heart and mind and give them hope for their future."

Tori wants others to know that there is life on the other side of addiction, even when their loved one does not recover.

"Yes, I went through a lot, but now I have a great life, I am going to school, have a good job, and Lily is so happy. I let my experience motivate me to never be that girl again."

2017 Update:

Tori is now working full time in a salon after graduating from school in September 2016. She has opened her heart to someone for the first time since David, and they have been together since February 2016. Lily is starting pre-school this spring to prepare for kindergarten next fall.

"We are very happy with where life is headed," she told me. "Everything is looking up."

Originally Published in the Daily Advertiser on December 17, 2015

MEET SANDY

Sandy wrote her brother's eulogy.

She spoke about how, when they were growing up, he was the "charmer," the stunningly handsome quarterback with the magnetic personality. She spoke about how he excelled at everything he did, from athletics to academics. She said her family would joke that he was so charismatic, he could charm his way out of anything.

And he did, until he couldn't.

Addiction doesn't care how charming you are.

Addiction doesn't care how book smart you are.

Addiction doesn't care how athletic you are.

Addiction doesn't care about your professional goals.

Addiction doesn't care if you are someone's little brother.

She cried as she penned it.

What some people may think is a bit strange though, is, *her brother is still alive.*

Sandy was so convinced she was going to lose him to addiction that she went as far as to write his eulogy; but he is still here.

There are many reasons why people fall into substance abuse in the first place.

Her brother, upon graduating from college, had plans to work for an international investment banking firm and coach baseball. All of that changed in an instant after he found himself in the ICU with myocarditis, an infection that directly attacks the heart. Fortunately, he recovered physically, but he never fully recovered mentally. He started having nightmares, and his anxiety escalated. He began self-medicating.

He slipped into a daily addiction. Those who suffer from addiction develop a high degree of skill for hiding their addiction, until the threads unravel. His addiction was brought to the surface two summers ago. Sandy was enjoying dinner with her brother, but he seemed "off."

When she brought up her concern, he told her he was just tired and had a bad day. Then, he started to "nod off"[23] at the table.

Sandy is a clinical social worker who works primarily with those with Substance Use Disorder and their families. She knew he was using.

She confronted him head-on with this, and he lost control. He became aggressive and condescending, pushed her aside, and left the restaurant.

"I realized right away that it was not my brother talking to me, but his addiction," she said.

---

[23] https://www.drugabuse.gov/publications/drugfacts/heroin

Sandy understood what it takes many families a long time to accept: this chronic illness will quickly engulf your loved one. It will take over their personality, their likeness, and their ability to be themselves.

Since that day, Sandy's life, as well as her brother's, has changed drastically. He has been through countless rehabs and one detox program, only to relapse again. He has gone missing for days, turning up with a broken hand, badly beaten and suffering from withdrawal. The police know his name. She has argued relentlessly with her parents, who she believes are enabling him to continue his destructive behavior.

"He lives with them. They pay his bills. He drives a car in their name," she explained.

Though she does place some blame on her parents for not adhering to what is best not only for her brother, but for her entire family, Sandy mostly blames herself.

"I blame myself every single day because my specialty is addiction, and I did not see the signs."

Sandy shared her story because she wants to reach other families who are going through a similar situation. Addiction is a family disease; every single person who loves a substance abuser is directly affected because they care. Addiction takes away a lot of things, but it does not take away a family's ability to care for their loved one. What addiction sometimes takes away, though, is the family's ability to care for themselves.

"I want families to know they are not alone," Sandy said. "You're not alone in having selfish thoughts."

Sandy set boundaries for herself early on to protect her mental and physical well-being. She wants families to know that setting boundaries is not selfish, but necessary, for survival.

If you love someone who is battling addiction, you will lose a lot of things: normalcy, time, your loved one, sleep and your sanity, but Sandy and I never want you to lose hope.

"There are days I have not wanted to get out of bed or even be in this world," Sandy admitted. "Yes, I have anxiety every time my phone rings, but you have to focus on hope. Even if they don't survive, you need to survive in spite of that."

Family members often ask themselves, "Is there any way out? Can he/she overcome the addiction in their life?"

The answer is yes, recovery is possible.

At the time of this interview in 2015, Sandy's brother was in recovery and "doing well." Because drug addiction actually changes your brain and body chemistry[24], it can take a long time for you to get back to normal emotionally, but he began to gain weight, attend therapy and regular support meetings with his sponsor, and receive medical treatment.

Millions of Americans are in long-term recovery[25], clean for years and decades. Sadly, many out there, including members of Sandy's own extended family, remain in the dark ages of ignorance when it comes to this disease.

---

[24]https://www.drugabuse.gov/publications/drugs-brains-behavior-science-addiction/drugs-brain

[25] http://www.recoveryanswers.org/resources/national/

Many act as though addiction is something one can "catch" simply by remaining in the same room as one who suffers.

Though her brother entered recovery, the stigma surrounding this illness remains. Many of her aunts, uncles, and cousins "shunned" Sandy because she remained supportive of her brother.

How many more premature eulogies need to be written before we all realize that those who suffer from addiction are doing just that: suffering? They are not simply weak or immoral. They are sick.

Drug addiction is an illness, and if anyone wants to argue that fact, they can take it up with the DSM, which is the definitive resource of diagnostic criteria for all mental disorders, or the American Society of Addiction Medicine (ASAM) that released a new definition of addiction after a four-year process involving more than 80 experts.[26]

"It's like my brother, my partner in crime, is back," she said. "I know that at any moment, my life can be turned upside down, so I try to enjoy every moment I have with him."

2017 Update:

It has been a tenuous period since I first shared Sandy's story.

---

[26] http://www.asam.org/quality-practice/definition-of-addiction

"At times I have felt I was going to have to use that eulogy I wrote," Sandy told me recently. "There also have been times that I could not imagine continuing myself. No one can imagine this hell."

Her brother has since relapsed and his drug use escalated to levels Sandy could never have anticipated. This has strained her relationship with her mother, and they do not speak for long periods.

"Some days, it feels like there is no end in sight. Other days, I feel so scared and my ability to function decreases. My anxiety has gotten completely out of control and I feel I make destructive decisions myself," she said.

"My family is still broken, and I grieve for people who are still alive, my own brother. No one can prepare you to lose people who are still alive. There is no closure, no goodbye, no end. Just a destructive cycle," she added.

The week before Christmas her brother called her; speaking fast and sounding disoriented.

The more he rambled, the more Sandy knew he wasn't clean.

"He hit me with the one/two punch," said Sandy. "He didn't get his fourth Vivitrol shot, and he gambled, winning over $1,500. I got off the phone and the pit in my stomach just got larger. I felt sick."

Sandy's brother would go on to cancel his next three appointments for his Vivitrol shot. Her phone stopped ringing.

"I tried to convince myself that this was not happening; that he didn't relapse before Christmas again. But I knew," Sandy wrote to me in an email.

Christmas Eve arrived, and Sandy reunited with her brother at their mother's house.

One look at him, and Sandy burst into tears – he had most definitely relapsed. He would spend the next 24 hours acting erratically, leaving the house, and spending long trips in the bathroom.

Christmas morning, he did not join his family to open presents, his pile of gifts remained wrapped. He showed up to Christmas dinner two hours late, then spent an hour in the bathroom.

He left the house Christmas night telling his girlfriend he would be by her within ten minutes. Ninety minutes passed and his girlfriend was still waiting for him.

"My mother told me that when she went to wake him on Christmas morning, there was cocaine and pills in his bed," recounted Sandy.

"I threw up. No mother should have to see that, least of all on Christmas morning," added Sandy. "Addiction has claimed more than one life in my family. It's literally killing us all. People say the Grinch stole Christmas. I say addiction did."

MEET MAUREEN

Before you continue reading, pull out your cell phone and retrieve the last text message you sent to a person you love. Read it out loud.

Maureen is a mother to a 23-year-old. Her most recent text message to her daughter, Ally, was, *Don't do heroin today.*

The one before that:

Do you have Narcan on you? Because you need it.

Her text messages weren't always this life-or-death, this worrisome, but like many families across the nation, this is her reality now.

Ally's upbringing was "normal." She grew up in a loving home with both parents and a brother just two years younger. Ally loved animals and playing outdoors. She had wild, curly brown hair and eyes to match. Her smile was contagious.

Then, it was as though the power went out behind her eyes, and her smile faded.

By 12, she was not the daughter Maureen knew. Her grades began to drop, and her behavior in school was getting her into trouble. Her friends changed. The happiness that once radiated from Ally was replaced by anger – *a lot of anger.*

Concerned for their daughter, Maureen and her husband brought Ally to a doctor who diagnosed her with having a Nonverbal Learning Disorder[27] and prescribed their 12-year-old Prozac.[28]

That didn't help, and not too long after, Ally tore her ACL while skiing. Ally, not yet a teenager, was administered Fentanyl, one of the strongest opiates out there, in the ambulance. The EMT told Maureen that he believed Ally "liked it too much."

After the Fentanyl in the ambulance and morphine at the hospital post-surgery, she began taking prescribed Percocet at home.[29]

This was all before Ally even entered high school.

After missing 40 days of school and still experiencing erratic, dangerous behavior at home, Ally was sent to a school that specialized with at-risk teens. She did extremely well there, earning straight A's.

After about a year, Maureen and her husband felt as though Ally was ready to come back and attend public high school.

By senior year, Ally was no longer living at home, was extremely thin, and dating someone who was nearly 20 years her senior. This man, who physically and mentally abused Ally, also introduced her to heroin.

---

[27]https://ldaamerica.org/types-of-learning-disabilities/non-verbal-learning-disabilities/

[28] https://www.drugwatch.com/prozac/

[29] https://www.drugs.com/percocet.html

Ever since, Ally has shortly found recovery only to relapse again, and fall even deeper into this murderous rabbit hole all too many of our youth are now spiraling down.

"I tell her that I love her, but I do not trust her," said Maureen.

Family members become warriors, advocates for change. They become humbled and find empowerment in their trauma, but they also spend countless hours questioning what they could have done differently.

"I've felt so much guilt," expressed Maureen. "I feel like if I had just done something...different...Ally would be okay. I believe God gave me Ally because he knows that I have faith, strength, and compassion to take care of my child who is also a child of God."

The longest Ally has been clean is two years.

Maureen has learned that all the faith in the world cannot save her daughter; only Ally can save Ally.

"She may never find recovery because she knows how to live on the streets," said Maureen, who sounded empty, hollow. "She thinks she is worthless. She does not believe she deserves recovery. And, she tells me she enjoys using heroin still."

She is now prostituting to support her habit. She has been evicted from her apartment. She has been arrested numerous times, having to detox without medical support in a jail cell.

Her body is failing, her kidneys are not functioning properly, her face is swollen, and she has been in and out of the hospital for bodily infections. All her belongings fit in one bag, and are usually stolen by other people living on the street.

This is not the life Maureen wanted for her daughter. This is not the life Maureen wanted for her family. Maureen has had to make the difficult decision not to allow her daughter to live at home.

"Some days the hardest thing I do is say, 'No you can't sleep at my house,'" admitted Maureen. "Or 'no, I cannot give you money.'"

Maureen and her husband still see their daughter regularly, dropping off care packages filled with first aid kits and fresh clothing.

"We saw her this past Sunday," Maureen told me. "Every time I hug her, I wonder if it will be the last. As I speak with you, I wonder if Sunday will end up being the last time I see my daughter alive."

As loved ones of substance abusers, for every "win" gained on this uphill battle, there are still stigmas attached that hurt not only the user, but the families involved.

"No one brings you casseroles when you have a child sick with addiction," said Maureen. "They bring you shame, judgment and their two cents of what they would have done to avoid my fate."

Maureen is quick to forewarn parents.

"Do not feel like you are a super parent who raised kids that cannot fall prey to this drug. Everyone is eligible to become a drug addict."

Her advice to parents and other loved ones in her shoes is to find a support group, be it Al-Anon or Nar-Anon.

"Choose your group wisely," she heeded. "A group that doesn't lead you to believe you have power over their addiction, because you do not."

Maureen and her husband attend support groups and manage to find comfort in knowing they are not alone in their unbearable pain and heartache.

"The best people are parents of other addicts," said Maureen. "If a person has an opinion on how to 'cure' drug addiction and they are not living through this or a medical professional, they should keep their uneducated opinions to themselves. If a person has a view on 'good parenting,' and they are not in my shoes as a parent of a drug addict, they should keep their opinion to themselves."

Maureen knows she sounds angry, but she is also of the belief that it is important to experience all stages of grief, especially anger.

"Sometimes you need to get angry. My anger led to my radical acceptance of my family's situation."

Maureen advocates for families directly affected by addiction and pushes for healthcare, like dental, wound cleaning, and blood pressure checks, to be available in the streets, where many users are living.

I asked Maureen what she thought would ultimately happen to her daughter.

"She will die soon if she does not find recovery."

2017 Update:

Maureen continues to worry for her daughter, who is still in active addiction and living on the streets.

"I saw my daughter on the day after Christmas and not since," Maureen told me, over email. "It is now about every two weeks that I may hear from her. She no longer has a telephone."

During her last visit, she tried to encourage her to get help. Her daughter is putting herself in danger with very dangerous people.

"I don't know what will happen next," stated Maureen. "More and more people at the shelter are carrying guns, and more people have died from overdoses in 2016 than in 2015 by me. We had an average of one a day, and that is sad."

"I hated figuring out that heroin was stronger than me," added Maureen. "I will be really devastated if she dies, but I don't honestly allow myself to think of that too often."

Originally Published on the Huffington Post on August 30, 2016

MEET LINDSEY

Within a six-month span in 2012, Lindsey lost three people to drug addiction. That's three dreaded phone calls, three worst nightmares, three funeral services, three times she felt like dying herself, three holes in her heart, all because of one drug. Heroin.

She lost Henry on April 23, 2012.

Henry, who was 24-years-old at the time, was Lindsey's first boyfriend, and they grew up together. Two years prior, Lindsey learned Henry, who excelled in political science in college, was using heroin. After many trips to rehab only to relapse, he hanged himself.

According to a 2014 report, people with substance use disorders are about six times more likely to commit suicide than the general population.[30]

"At his memorial, I spoke of all the amazing adventures we had together," said Lindsey. "All I really wanted was to scream and curse 'WHY?' But you can't say things like that at a funeral."

Tragedy struck Lindsey's family three months later when her cousin, Joey, who she considered a brother, overdosed.

---

[30]http://www.psychiatrictimes.com/substance-use-disorder/link-between-substance-abuse-violence-and-suicide

"He must have felt like he was having an asthma attack because he died trying to plug in his nebulizer," said Lindsey.

Joey lived with Lindsey's family, sharing a room with Lindsey, for five years of his life. Lindsey knew he was battling a pill addiction and had been to rehab twice, but did not know Joey was addicted to heroin until after he died.

Lindsey still has the last text message he sent her on July 6, 2012: *I love you.*

He died the next day. He was just 18-years-old.

Leo, a close friend of Lindsey's, overdosed and died on October 30, 2012.

Lindsey discovered Leo was using three years prior when she caught him with a local heroin dealer. Lindsey was shocked since Leo's own stepfather had overdosed and died earlier in Leo's life.

Leo's mother asked Lindsey to put together the memory boards for his services. He was 25-years-old at the time of his death.

"I knew this would happen," admitted Lindsey. "Sad reality, but most people battling this addiction do not make it."

Lindsey and the three loved ones she's lost all grew up and lived in a very small town in Upstate New York. Lindsey began grammar school and graduated from high school with the same 60 students.

Everyone knew everyone, so when Lindsey experienced her loss, she was not alone. The entire community was affected by the deaths of these three young men. Yet, that has not stopped people from using heroin in her town.

"So many here are still using," confessed Lindsey. "Some of them I have known forever, some of them are related to people who have already died. I am still surrounded by it, but these days, who isn't?"

Lindsey is right. The United States is struggling with a heroin epidemic, with the number of users reaching a 20-year high, according to a United Nations report.[31] Cincinnati is in the news this week for a bad batch of heroin that led to an "unprecedented" 174 overdoses in just six days. Reports are stating the heroin at the root of the overdose surge is cut with carfentanil, an elephant tranquilizer, 10,000 times stronger than morphine.[32]

Like many out there, Lindsey believes her generation is struggling with this drug because of the availability of painkillers. Studies have proven the connection. Whether the pills were rightfully prescribed or not, many become hooked and begin buying them on the streets. A prescription pill habit can quickly become too costly to maintain, so many turn to heroin because it is far cheaper, and maybe still surprising to some, easier to find.[33]

---

[31] http://www.reuters.com/article/us-drugs-usa-heroin-idUSKCN0Z90UX

[32] http://www.mnn.com/family/protection-safety/blogs/what-carfentanil

[33] http://www.narconon.org/blog/heroin-addiction/5-reasons-prescription-addiction-turns-to-heroin/

"2012 was the worst year of my life," stated Lindsey, matter-of-factly. "There were so many days that year where I would lay down at night and not even remember the day I just had. I was too preoccupied with death and the decisions these three made."

Lindsey fell into a deep depression and even contemplated taking her life. She credits her mother and her best friend for keeping her head above water during those dark moments.

"I made the decision with my doctor to go on depression medication while I was going through this," explained Lindsey. "It helped me get through the worst of it, after a year and counseling, I was able to learn to cope without antidepressants."

Lindsey, now 27, has begun to focus on one of her life goals, a dream that got pushed to the side as she worked through her nightmare and grief: graduate school.

"I am happy to say that after four years and countless attempts I am finally enrolled in a master's program!" announced Lindsey, who hopes to become a school counselor one day.

"It has taken me four years to try and deal with all of these emotions, and it still takes a toll on me every day. Depression takes a hold, and when that happens, all I can do is hope for a better tomorrow."

Lindsey has learned first-hand that you cannot love someone out of addiction. Her advice to other people who love someone struggling with Substance Use Disorder is to ask for help, both from your friends and family as well as doctors and counselors, when feeling overwhelmed with helplessness.

"Remember to always tell them you love them," stressed Lindsey. "Do not end of conversation without saying 'I love you.' It's more for you, than for them, because believe me, you do not want to the last words you say to be anything but 'I love you.'"

2017 Update:

The brother of Lindsey's best friend Leo, who died October 30, 2012, was recently hospitalized with injuries and infection related to using heroin.

"I check in with him daily just to remind him that there are people who love him and care, also I guess I want our last conversation to be one of love, not disappointment and anger like it was with his brother," said Lindsey. "Every day his wife, his mother, and his son, along with all of his friends, worry that today could be the last day, it's terrifying and unfair, but that's what this addiction is...terrifying and unfair."

Since being hospitalized, he was diagnosed with Bipolar Disorder[34], was kicked out of his house, and the only person who would take him in was his old caseworker who managed to talk him into therapy.

He's now on medication for his disorder and he has managed to stay clean since the day he was admitted to the hospital.

---

[34] https://www.nimh.nih.gov/health/topics/bipolar-disorder/index.shtml

"He can talk about why he used, and I've never seen him this calm and together! Finally!" exclaimed Lindsey. "It feels like there is some hope for him to fight this disease!"

Originally Published on the Huffington Post September 23, 2016

MEET ELLEN

Ellen is grieving the loss of her son. She has removed the framed pictures of the 19-year-old from the walls of her home. She's tucked away photo albums and removed pictures from beneath the magnets of her refrigerator. She's taken down his childhood artwork that froze his little hands in time, and has removed his telephone number from her phone. His bedroom door remains closed. This is how Ellen is coping.

The only thing is, her son cannot be found in any cemetery. In fact, Ellen has no idea where her son is sleeping tonight, but he is alive.

Ellen describes her son as a "challenging, but very unique" boy.

"Growing up, some people called our son prodigal, because his musical talent was pretty extreme," said Ellen.

By the age of 10, he was composing original pieces on the piano. He could pick up any instrument, even a bagpipe, and play it well. He loved butterflies, flowers, singing, and bluegrass music.

What set him apart caused him to be bullied in school, with many of his peers spewing homophobic slurs in his direction. His peers would continue to misunderstand him all the way through high school, and this resulted in her son rebelling.

"By his sophomore year, he had been caught plagiarizing and cheating on tests. He was suspended twice. We moved him to a bigger high school, 60 miles away from home," said Ellen. "To attend this school, he had to ride the bus for three hours, round trip. We thought this school, being bigger, more diverse, could offer him a new social environment to help him find his voice."

"We took him to naturopaths, neuropsychologists, doctors, alternative medical professionals to try and help him focus in school and cope with his unique personality," added Ellen.

Changing schools and seeking treatment did not resolve her son's issues. He continued to struggle with his identity, jumping in and out of numerous social circles, donning new clothes and different tastes in music every two weeks. His grades started to drop, and he found himself in trouble with numerous teachers. This was when he began smoking e-cigarettes and marijuana.

"He became violent and combative, and increased his ability to lie compulsively," said Ellen, describing her son's textbook behavior. "He hacked into our eBay account and began spending thousands of dollars. He built an ethanol still[35] in our attic and nearly blew the place up."

He was 15 when he first got into trouble with the law and had to complete community service.

---

[35] http://environment.about.com/od/ethanolfaq/f/what_is_ethanol.htm

Ellen knew her son was experimenting with drugs like marijuana, hash oil[36], and possibly prescription pills, and began searching his bedroom regularly, destroying any paraphernalia she found.

Shortly after Ellen confronted her son, he ran away from home, a few weeks' shy of his 18th birthday.

"He drove off in a rainstorm in his 1928 model T Ford. He even filed an abuse and neglect claim with Child Protective Services," recalled Ellen. "He barely kept himself alive for the rest of the school year. He couch-surfed until he managed to rent a dive studio apartment above a bar. We attempted family therapy together as well as one-on-one counseling."

Ten days before his high school graduation, he was caught shooting at pedestrians with a BB gun from his apartment. He spent three days in jail. He was first sentenced with two felonies, but the charges were dropped to misdemeanors.

Six months later, the charges were re-instated in district court. He pled guilty to two counts of felony assault.

Ellen's routine is anything but routine, but it has become her norm. She reads the newspapers obsessively, flipping right to the *Crime and Court* section. She routinely checks for her son's name in the city jail roster online. She flinches each time an unfamiliar phone number appears on her phone. She dreads a sheriff's call, the coroner's call. She has become all too familiar with the numbing, unmistakable sound of the prison phone line.

---

36 http://www.a1b2c3.com/drugs/hash003.htm

"I've taken to checking my Facebook page just to see if my son's been online in the last 12 hours," said Ellen. "When more than 10 hours pass without any noticeable online activity, I start to worry that he is in the hospital, the morgue, or in some overdosed puddle of vomit and blood."

Her son's downward spiral and addictions have ruined his young life.

"He is now serving a three-year deferred sentence. He has to register as a violent offender in every county that he spends more than 72 hours in," explained Ellen. "He cannot vote, get a passport, travel beyond the state line, or get a car loan. He has paid thousands of dollars in court fines and completed dozens of community service hours. He cannot apply for many jobs because of his felony convictions."

There are nearly 27 conditions of his probation, including, of course, strict terms against using drugs and alcohol, yet his cell phone records lead Ellen to believe her son is regularly dealing drugs, regardless of the circumstances of his probation.

Parents will hear time and time again that they cannot love their children out of their addiction. Parents will hear time and time again that the decision to enter a program and recover must come from within the user. Parents will hear time and time again, that regardless of the fates of their children, they must take the appropriate steps to recover, too. Parents will hear time and time again that accepting all of this is easier said than done, and maybe even impossible.

"The fact that he no longer is part of our lives is just devastating," said Ellen. "When other parents complain about their children, I find a bitterness welling up in my heart. I want to yell, 'At least your child isn't a felon! At least he isn't homeless, eating out of the Taco Bell dumpster! At least he isn't facing three years of strict probation in a small city where just about everyone knows his name!'"

Ellen receives little sympathy for her son's disease. Instead, she collects cold shoulders, hurtful whispers, and judging stares.

"I've felt stigmatized every fucking day since he turned 14," said Ellen. "We have lost multiple friends. People were horrified by the news, the newspaper articles, the radio, the child protective services visits. People have made judgments about us that will never change. No one can understand the hurt this causes, as if we haven't been drowning in pools of private hurt and guilt for the last five years!"

Sadly, many fellow parents can commiserate with Ellen. A quick Google of the phrase "parents with drug addicted child" yields more than 40 million results in a mere two seconds.[37]

"I hope other parents can learn that they aren't alone, that other people are going through similar situations with their families, their children," expressed Ellen. "I hope other parents going through this decide not to hide, withdraw, or remove themselves from their communities."

---

[37]https://www.google.com/search?q=parents+with+drug+addicted+child&rlz=1C1C AFA_enUS687US687&oq=parents+with+drug+addicted+child&aqs=chrome..69i57. 518j0j4&sourceid=chrome&ie=UTF-8

In Ellen's case, she still has hope, though it is dwindling with each passing day where she does not receive a phone call from her son, the once-promising musician.

"I'd like to think that he can crawl out of this deep, cold grave that he has dug for himself. My dreams for him were as big as his own dreams before he drowned them in whatever poison he feeds on these days," said Ellen. "We never imagined this. Our family is broken, shattered. I'm devastated, depressed, and withdrawn. We are grieving for our boy, our family. We miss him, and love him, and hurt so very much for him."

Originally Published on the Huffington Post on December 28, 2015

THE J-WORD

"Fuck junkies. It's disgusting. What lowlifes."

Thursday morning began like all of my other Thursday mornings. I was at Starbucks. I wanted a Venti Iced Chai Latte because it tastes like Christmas. The line was long; two women in tailored suits and pumps were chatting in front of me. The newspaper rack caught one of their attentions, and she nudged her friend toward the headline without picking the paper up.

That's when she said it. One of the only words that can make me visibly cringe.

My eyes darted to the headline. It was highlighting New Jersey's widespread heroin problem. There weren't even any pictures for her to draw her uneducated conclusion; just a cheesy, antiquated stock photo of a needle and a spoon.

I bit my lower lip like I usually do when I try to keep my mouth shut. "Excuse me," I interjected, politely. "How do you know I'm not a heroin addict?"

She stared blankly at me, speechless, so her friend answered for her, "You don't look like one."

I stopped being polite. "I know 'one' who looks just like you."

We need to stop using the word "junkie" when referring to those who are battling addiction. I want human beings to feel shame if they slip and use the "J" word. Because, simply put, its use is doing nothing to help the cause.

I consider it a slur, much like a homophobic, body-shaming, or racial slur, because by definition, that is what it is. The Merriam-Webster Dictionary defines the word "slur" as "an insinuation or allegation about someone that is likely to insult them or damage their reputation."

As a writer, I know the words we choose to use matter. The use of derogatory words like "junkie" or "dope fiend" not only greatly affects the drug user's psyche, but those who care deeply for them as well.

Yes, I am not addicted to drugs, but when I heard those two girls throw around that slur so easily, it messed up my entire day. I wanted to scream. I wanted to cry. I wanted to sit them down and present to them a PowerPoint presentation on this disease.

The use of such negative language decreases people who use drugs to a stigmatized stereotype. Not to mention, it is discriminatory, patronizing and challenges the public understanding of people who use drugs and the issues they face whether in long-term recovery or actively using.

Addiction slurs invoke such graphic images, most of which are outdated and without merit. Many still do not realize one does not need to inject heroin in order to use heroin.[38]

---

[38] http://headsup.scholastic.com/students/drug-facts-heroin

How can so many still believe there is a clear divide between who uses drugs and who doesn't? I have spoken to numerous families who have experienced this disease and the only thing these people have in common - the only common thread between them all - is addiction.

I spoke with Adrianne and Mike, from New York. They lost their son, Justin, to addiction earlier this month and have jumped right into the advocacy ring, even noting his battle with addiction in his obituary.

"When I hear the word 'junkie' I think of the stereotypical shooting up and nodding out in the streets," said Adrianne. "The reality is it affects people of all social and economic standings."

Every family affected by addiction come from different backgrounds, cities and states, are different ages, hold down various occupations, fall into varying tax brackets, and have different religious affiliations.

The word "junkie" encapsulates every single person who combats this sickness into one outmoded stereotype without even taking into consideration who the person even was before falling into addiction.

"No one tried any kind of drug and said 'I want to be an addict'," Adrianne continued. "It's a disease, but unlike other diseases, there is little sympathy for an addict."

Everyone was a child once, including those battling addiction. They wanted to be astronauts and ballerinas when they grew up, not prisoners to their own addictions. They believed in Santa Clause.

They never rooted for the "bad guy" to win in their morning cartoons. When they pledged in elementary school to "just say no," they meant it.

They didn't talk to strangers, and couldn't predict that one day they'd be purchasing life threatening substances from them.

Like many of us, they believed in right and wrong. Addiction drives many to do reprehensible things, with many breaking the law to support their habit, but these aren't bad people; *these are sick people.*

When did we as a society become so jaded that we forgot, or choose to ignore, that these people are still living breathing people who need help?

"The ignorance infuriates me," said Laurel, a professional in the addiction and recovery field.

Laurel has spent the last seven years devoting her life to addiction recovery. She holds a license as a Clinical Alcohol and Drug Counselor and is currently working as a Care Coordinator, conducting assessments for clients who many need substance and/or mental health treatment. "People are choosing to avoid learning about why addiction is a disease and want to reach their conclusions based on opinion instead of scientific fact. It is not about comparing all physical diseases to addiction; it's about understanding how addiction impairs the user and shows signs and symptoms, just like every other illness."

Prior to taking on the role as Care Coordinator, Laurel spent over five years as a counselor and Clinical Supervisor in an outpatient setting, where she heard many people refer to themselves "Junkies."

She concludes this is because they have had people continually speak down to them and label them as such, and in turn, they began to see themselves as inferior. Laurel tells me that it's a vicious cycle, and suggests that the addiction is actually exacerbated by the stigma.

"By reframing the way we speak about anyone with a disability, like saying 'he has been diagnosed with Bipolar Disorder' instead of blankly stating, 'he's a Bipolar,' or 'she is struggling with addiction' instead of 'she's just another junkie,' it reminds us to think about the person first," explained Laurel. "By being willing to learn about addiction, we will help change the perspective of those who judge, label, and demean."

At this point, everyone knows someone who has been directly affected by addiction. The National Institute of Health recently came out and said we are "dealing with the dynamics of a disease that sometimes requires as much investment from family and community as it does from the individual struggling to recover."[39]

In response, families have stood up and nonprofit organizations have been formed to help combat these stigmas. I spoke with Rick Rosenhagen Jr., the president of Heroin Support Incorporation, a 501c3 based out of Kentucky.

---

[39] https://medlineplus.gov/magazine/issues/spring07/articles/spring07pg14-17.html

"People need to get educated on addiction, so that we can change the stigma surrounding the social label of 'junkie'. Addiction is a disease that changes the functionality and structure of the brain. Most users hate the life they live each day," said Rick.

The world is shaped by the language we use. Using a word like "junkie," even just to your friend, only facilitates continued ignorance about this epidemic and continues to blur people into a stereotype. Those who are battling addiction are not one-dimensional fictional characters; they are supremely real human beings who are suffering every single day.

Stop calling them "junkies." *They have first names.*

Learn more about Heroin Support, Inc.:

www.facebook.com/heroinkillsyou

MEET JUSTIN
(September 10, 1973 - December 6, 2015)

In the previous story, you met Adrianne, whose son Justin lost his battle with drugs. This is an email I received from Adrianne on the one-year anniversary of Justin's death. Reprinted with permission.

Many people thought they knew Justin. They saw the addict. They didn't see the man behind the disease.

The few who remained in his life, those few faithful friends, and family, knew the *real Justin*. Justin loved music, art, nature, sushi, a good steak, and a hot shower. He was an avid reader who read books that most couldn't fathom or understand. He watched the History channel and the science channel and was brilliant.

He loved animals. He cared for the underdog. A girl, who attended high school with Justin, wrote to me after he passed, telling me a story about his kindness to her when everyone else treated her as an outcast.

When he finally had gotten a job those last weeks of his life, he told me about a girl who was being mistreated because she was overweight. He felt sorry for her, and he said he talked to her and tried to help her not be intimidated by them. He had a very kind heart.

All his past jobs were in service; the County working with at-risk kids, the Center for Discovery working with that population, Harlem Children's Zone, where he once carried a piece of furniture on his back to deliver it to a family in need.

He loved passionately, and he hated passionately. You never had to question where you stood with Justin. He was loyal to a fault. He was also very sensitive, and he thought that everyone was loyal like he was, and had his heart broken many times as people he thought cared about him, turned their backs on him in his times of need.

So, when you think of Justin, I ask that you try to focus on the man he was; the loving grandson, nephew, cousin, and friend, and not the disease...the addiction.

It is a year now since we lost our boy, our only child. It is a nightmare no parent should have to bear. We are, and will be, forever grateful to the many, many people who have offered their love and friendship to us. Even people who didn't know us, or him, well or at all. It means the world to us.

Justin will forever be alive in our hearts.

-Adrianne
Justin's Mother

MEET PETER

The more articles I write about addiction, the more emails I receive from strangers all over the country.

On January 9, 2016, I received an email with the subject line "A Sad Dad..."

I knew what the email would say before I opened it. By now, I know of far too many "sad dads" across our nation who lost children to drug addiction.

This father's name is Peter. In 2012, he lost his 21-year-old daughter Nicole, "Nikki," to drug addiction.

I am not yet a parent. I will not even begin to try to relate to what parents go through when they lose a child, regardless of the circumstances; but I sat in the chair beside my aunt at my cousin's funeral for two days, and those images still break me.

I went home in 2006 and scribbled in one of my journals, *Sit next to a person who lost a child and you will see that life can kill you every single day without ever burying you.*

Now, Peter's email to me was short, it simply read:

Hello, Alicia. All of our sad stories sound the same after a while, but they aren't the same. Sincerely, Peter.

However, Peter had provided me with an attachment.

It was the eulogy he read at his daughter's funeral.

You may share the attached
if you think it will help somebody.

Heroin is a national concern, killing more of us annually than automobile accidents.[40]

I opened the attachment and began to read the eulogy. I stopped in shock by the third paragraph.

"There are many funny stories I can share with you about Nikki, but I am not going to do that today," I read. "Instead, I have something even more important to speak to you about – drugs, narcotics, and whatever other names they go by. I have come up with a very fitting name for the drugs that end up in the hands of our children – *poison*."

Peter, a grieving father, used this eulogy to forewarn Nikki's peers, sitting in the church benches, about the dangers and repercussions of drug abuse.

No one can use heroin in a recreational way. As more and more families take a stand against the heroin epidemic, I have seen obituaries attack this head-on; they don't coast over it with the ambiguous "died suddenly" phrase anymore.

Families want to help other families feel less alone in their struggle and loss. Families want to see changes to public policy.

Peter wanted to help other families not suffer the same fate as his family.

---

[40]https://www.washingtonpost.com/news/wonk/wp/2015/12/17/guns-are-now-killing-as-many-people-as-cars-in-the-u-s/?utm_term=.8c928b38054a

"Heroin took the life of my Nikki," I continued reading. "It managed to enter her life, addict her, take control of her mind, make her sick, and finally kill her."

I spoke with Peter after reading the eulogy. Nikki was one of three children Peter had with his wife, Anne. She had a twin sister and a younger brother. She loved cats, movies, ice cream, and reading. She was beautiful and full of life.

"Everyone that knew her, loved her," Peter reminisced, once I reached out to him. "She had more friends than the four of us combined."

Nikki was tiny; all of five feet tall and 100 pounds, but fearless. She was also completely loyal to her siblings, standing up for them countless times.

Peter mentioned to me a time when Nikki barged into where her sister's ex-boyfriend worked to confront him about cheating on her twin. I smiled when he told me that, because my sister would, and has, done the same for me.

Peter and his wife cannot pinpoint why or when Nikki started using drugs. The family believes Nikki turned to drugs after being sexually molested at 16 (she did not tell her family about this until much later), and following the suicide of a good friend.

She was using, they estimate, nearly two years before they were able to isolate the problem and get her to a hospital and into a program.

"When she came out of rehab, she was okay. I swear she was," he said. He sounded like he was trying to not only convince me, but himself.

Things were seemingly better for Nikki and her family again for nearly another two years.

"She was a hair stylist. She was building up a clientele. She was living home surrounded with love from her family and friends."

After five years of rehabs, hospitals, detox programs, therapists, and doctor-prescribed medications, Nikki lost her battle with substance abuse one day after her 21st birthday.

To this day, Peter believes she wanted to recover, but just couldn't find the right help for herself.

"She was looking for outlets to replace her addiction. She started hiking, making jewelry, reading and writing poetry, and became interested in learning to play the guitar."

Peter hopes sharing Nikki's story and the eulogy he delivered will help young people understand that drugs re-wire your brain, making addiction, and then death, inevitable.

"I want them to know that they are not invincible, as most of us like to believe at a young age. I want our young people to know that they will cause a great deal of pain to their family. I want our young people to know drugs won't make problems disappear. I want them to know that their best defense, probably the only defense, against becoming addicted to drugs is to never, ever try them."

Peter has regrets. Nikki was lying to her family a lot toward the end, making it hard to believe what she was saying.

"She left this world thinking that her father didn't believe the awful things that happened to her, and this hurts me deeply."

Because of this, Peter wants to stress to other parents going through a similar situation: "Listen to your children. Offer them tangible support, not just lip service like 'it's just a part of growing up' or 'you'll be fine' because they might not be fine."

When he told me this, I almost cried.

I thought back to my cousin's funeral and witnessing my uncle slip a $10 bill into the front pocket of the shirt they had picked out for her. At the time, I asked him why.

He had told me, "For the last year of her life I couldn't give her any money because I couldn't trust what she was going to spend it on."

Peter's advice to other parents is to not take every single bit of advice.

"Follow your own heart. I heard the term 'tough love' a lot when Nikki was deep into her addiction. One example of tough love is to throw the addict out on the street," he began. "Right, wrong, or indifferent, I was not going to throw her out. If she was going to die, she was going to die with us, and not in some alleyway, away from the people who loved her the most."

The eulogy ended like how I imagine many eulogies delivered by grieving parents conclude.

"I want to thank God for lending Nikki to us for 21 wonderful years. It pains me to know that she will never experience many of the joys in life like feeling the love of a husband, raising children, and being the Maid of Honor at her twin sister's wedding."

THE EULOGY

Unedited. Reprinted with permission.

Greetings All, first I'd like to thank you all for taking time out of your busy lives to spend a few hours with my family today. I've probably never met many of you, but I know you had some kind of connection with my beloved daughter Nicole. And I thank you all from the bottom of my heart for being with us today. Your presence is needed and very much appreciated.

And before I forget if any of you have any fond memories of your time spent with Nicole, please post them to her Facebook, if you haven't done so already. I haven't had the strength yet to read the posts, but I'm looking forward to reading every word from every one of you. Also, if you have extra copies of photos of you with Nicole please pass them along. I would very much enjoy looking at them.

I've always considered myself more of a listener than a talker, and I am certainly not the type of guy who speaks in front of a crowd. But I have a few things I need to say today for Nicole, and I would do anything for her, including speaking in front of a crowd of people.

There are many funny stories that I can share with you about Nikki, but I am not going to do that today. Instead, I have something even more important to speak to you about – DRUGS, NARCOTICS, and whatever other names they go by. I have come up with a very fitting name for all of the different kinds of street drugs that circulate out there and somehow end up in the hands of many of our children – POISON.

In case some of you don't know, one poison in particular, also referred to as Heroin, took the life of my Nikki. It managed to enter her life, addict her, take control of her mind and many of her actions, make her sick, and finally kill her. It transformed her from a beautiful, healthy, confident, and outgoing young lady, into a frail, broken-out, introverted sick girl who had come to believe, albeit wrongfully so, that she was a failure and had no friends.

Nicole's mother and I did all we could, right up until the end, to save her from her sickness of addiction. Nikki had been in and out of hospitals, detox centers, out-patient rehabs, drug-education classes, therapists' offices, and she had tried many different types of doctor-prescribed medications. These were all un-successful.

The poison's hold on her was too powerful.

I'd like to address the teens and the twentysomethings here today. I'm here to say that drugs are not recreation or problem solvers. Simply put, drugs will make you sick and can kill you.

Never turn to them, ever!

If you are feeling down because you didn't do as well as you thought you did on a test, didn't get the job that you really wanted, or didn't get the time of day from the boy or girl that you really had a crush on – then call a friend. Go to a movie. Read a book. Go hiking. But just be patient, because you'll ace the next test, get an even better job, or meet the boy or girl that was really meant for you.

And if, Heaven forbid, you are currently having a problem with drugs. Don't delay, talk to your parents, grandparents, siblings, and any other loved ones. Trust them. Don't be afraid of what their initial reaction will be. They'll be emotional at first, but then they'll get right to work at seeking out the help you need. Nikki didn't do this. Nikki kept things from us because she didn't want to hurt us or have us worry about her. She told us the things that we wanted to hear and not the things that were really going on with her. We had to figure out these things on our own and we lost precious time because of it.

To all of you parents out there, if your son or daughter is having a problem with drugs. Never stop fighting for them, no matter how hopeless the situation may appear. If it becomes exhausting, get a good night's sleep, and wake up swinging the next day. We never stopped fighting for Nicole, right to the end, and we would have never stopped fighting for her.

In closing, I know my Nikki is with God today because even though her mind and body were ravaged by this disease, her heart remained pure and her devotion to God never faltered. And this brings me peace. I also want to thank you God for lending Nikki to us for 21 wonderful years. And even though I know I will see her again one day, I am broken-hearted. Because she left us at such a young age, it pains me to know that she will never experience many of the joys in life like feeling the warmth and love of a husband, having the privilege of raising children of her own, and being the maid-of-honor at her twin sister Ashley's wedding.

I love you and will miss you my darling daughter until we meet again in heaven.

Thank you and may God bless you all.

MEET RACHEL

Rachel was 12-years-old when she learned her cousin and most trusted confidante, Jeremy, was dependent on heroin.

It wasn't until five years later, in 2015, that Jeremy actually admitted he was addicted to heroin, though. The admission was brought on after Jeremy survived his first heroin overdose.

Jeremy entered, and completed, rehab and returned home.

"My cousin was always the life of the party; the funniest person I've ever met. Girls loved him," described Rachel. "I never noticed how much he and I drifted apart until he began his journey to recovery and I got the old Jeremy back. I had my best friend back that I never even realized I lost."

Like many families who experience a loved one's first successful stint in rehab, Rachel and her family believed the hardest part was behind Jeremy; he was recovered, and their family could transition back to their normal lives and routines.

"This being my family's first time going down the road of recovery with somebody, we thought we had it covered," admitted Rachel. "We'll monitor him, babysit him, never let him be alone, and nothing will ever happen."

Unfortunately, the National Institute on Drug Abuse states that between 40% and 60% of recovering drug users will eventually relapse. With heroin, those rates are even higher. Some experts claim the rate of relapse for those addicted to heroin is as high as 80%, which means that the recovery rate may be as low as 20%.[41]

Jeremy and Rachel grew up very close, living right next door to one another. Rachel was "over the moon" that her cousin was clean and himself once again. Jeremy was home from rehab for 15 days when he and Rachel decided to partake in a beloved, little tradition of theirs at home: ice cream and milkshakes.

After excusing himself to use the bathroom, Jeremy returned shortly after, visibly high, and collapsed right in front of Rachel. He began seizing on the floor, his breathing hollow, his skin turning blue. Rachel and Jeremy were home alone, and he was dying right in front of her eyes.

"I was 17-years-old at the time and in that moment I had every bit of innocence ripped from me when I looked at his face and thought, 'I don't know what is happening, but he's going to die if I don't do something,'" recalled Rachel. "I was all alone and he put me in that situation."

Rachel called 911 and Jeremy's mother. Both responded to the house immediately. Narcan was administered, and Jeremy survived his second overdose. As he was being rolled to the ambulance, he spewed hateful things at Rachel. By then, Rachel knew that was the addiction talking, not Jeremy.

---

[41] http://crehab.org/blog/addiction/what-are-the-addiction-recovery-rates-for-heroin/

"I think back to that night every day, and I get so angry," said Rachel. "How could the one person, who was never supposed to hurt me, hurt me more than anyone ever will?"

A question posed by families across the nation.

Jeremy entered rehab again but did not complete the program. He then moved into a sober house for five months. A year later, Jeremy still struggles daily with his heroin addiction, staying clean only to relapse time and time again.

Rachel feels as though Jeremy does not have much remorse for what he put her through the day they were making milkshakes because he has repeated the behavior of using when they are alone together.

"He says he wants to stay clean, but does not want to go to rehab," said Rachel. "He claims completing rehab that one time was enough and he just needs to utilize the coping skills he learned there."

"Jeremy claims he understands that his problem has a direct effect on everybody, yet he tells us his problem is not our problem," added Rachel. "I'm at the point now where I am totally convinced he'll never stop using drugs and it saddens me that I even think that. Most of the time I really believe he doesn't care that he's hurting us."

Rachel, now 18, is still trying to wrap her head around how someone like Jeremy, now 29, could have drugs continue to ruin his life, and the lives of those who care about him most.

Six years of Rachel's life has been spent worrying if her cousin was going to die. A rational fear of many who love someone battling the disease of addiction.

Rachel still considers Jeremy her best friend. They talk and/or see each other every day, but Rachel admits that his relapses are a constant strain on their relationship.

"I've had nightmares about the night Jeremy overdosed. To this day, I'm nervous to be alone with him. It was a learning experience, but it was also completely traumatizing," expressed Rachel. "It's heartbreaking to think I can't trust someone I once trusted with my life. This is a painful, everyday struggle and I would give my life for Jeremy to get better. I just want the life we had with him 10 years ago back."

Originally Published on Addiction Unscripted on January 4, 2017

MEET DANIELLE

Danielle is 37-years-old, and a widow.

Her husband, Greg, passed away 10 months ago, on March 5, 2016, leaving behind Danielle and their two young boys.

Their love story began just following September 11, 2001. Danielle and Greg were both in the military. They met and fell in love fast when he was on leave from the Marine Corp. Danielle left for the Air Force soon after meeting Greg and the two maintained a long distance relationship, exchanging letters and speaking on the phone.

Greg was slated for deployment to Iraq but was injured, paralyzing his foot, while training in Japan and was discharged. Greg moved to where Danielle was stationed. They got married and, soon after, Danielle discovered she was pregnant with their first child.

"He was amazing," said Danielle. "He cooked, cleaned, and was so romantic. He would get up and make me breakfast every day and iron my uniform. He was unlike any other man I ever met."

Now a disabled Marine, Greg went back to college, earned his second bachelor's degree, and became an elementary special education teacher, working with children with Autism.

After four years, Danielle was out of the Air Force, their little family moved, and Greg secured another teaching position. Greg received the "Rookie Teacher of the Year" award at the conclusion of his first year there, beating out all other first-year teachers in the entire school district.

Two years later, they relocated again when Danielle was hired by the FAA, and they welcomed their second son nearly five years into their marriage. That is around the time Danielle began to notice changes in her doting husband's behavior.

As our nation has come to rely more heavily on pharmaceutical drugs, the U.S. military has followed suit, prescribing drugs on both the battlefield and home front in a vast network of V.A. hospitals and clinics.[42]

Veterans taking prescribed drugs may become dependent and spiral into full-blown addiction.

Since being injured in Japan, Greg remained on a wide variety of prescribed pain pills (opiates), as well as Adderall[43] and Xanax[44], the entire fourteen years of their marriage.

"I would notice him nodding off," recalled Danielle. "Then one time he ran to the store with my son and after they returned he passed out in his truck while it was still running. One day, when he was really messed up, I dropped him off at rehab."

---

[42] https://www.addictioncenter.com/addiction/veterans/

[43] https://www.drugs.com/adderall.html

[44] https://www.drugs.com/xanax.html

For the majority of Greg's time overusing pain medication, Danielle did not tell anyone, even their own family.

"Only a handful of friends and family knew the struggles in our household. Most had no idea that the boys and I had spent the previous two Christmases alone. They didn't know the hours we spent at the doctor's office trying to find the right drugs and balance."

The first time Greg entered rehab, it was to get off Xanax.

When people become addicted to Xanax, they cannot escape it without experiencing painful withdrawal. In fact, it is so painful and harmful, that Xanax withdrawal has been linked to death. Users can shock their systems if they try to stop taking Xanax cold turkey[45], so a supervised weaning off of the drug is encouraged.[46]

Rehab didn't help. Danielle would come home late from work to find her husband passed out and the house a mess. Her children would tell her they hadn't eaten dinner.

"Even during all of that, I never really thought of him as a drug addict," she said. "To me, drug addicts were people who stole from their loved ones and lived on the streets. Addicts weren't people who got their drugs from a doctor."

"We were working together, as a couple, with his pain management doctor to find a happy balance between him and myself," added Danielle.

---

[45] http://www.dictionary.com/browse/cold-turkey

[46] http://americanaddictioncenters.org/xanax-treatment/dangers-cold-turkey/

It didn't work. The second time Greg entered rehab, it was for opiates that were being prescribed by his doctor. He got out of another 30-day treatment center and got his prescription filled before his doctor could find out.

Greg received a shot of Vivitrol, but lied about receiving the second shot. Danielle was unaware of this until the first time Greg overdosed on a combination of morphine[47] and Seroquel.[48] He also had marijuana, benzodiazepines (Xanax), and amphetamines[49] in his system.

Xanax is considered to be more toxic than other benzodiazepines. In one study published by the British Journal of Pharmacology, the length of stay for 131 people who overdosed on Xanax was 1.27 times longer than people who overdosed on other "benzos." Of those who overdosed on Xanax, 22% were treated in intensive care units – 2.06 times more than other cases.[50]

"I was stunned and embarrassed when the doctor asked me if I knew my husband had been shooting up," admitted Danielle. "I thought he had gotten the second Vivitrol shot. I thought he was only on a nerve pill."

Danielle learned Greg had been "double dipping" between the V.A. and his pain doctor.

---

[47] https://www.drugs.com/morphine.html

[48] https://www.drugs.com/seroquel.html

[49] http://www.druginfo.adf.org.au/drug-facts/amphetamines

[50] https://www.ncbi.nlm.nih.gov/pmc/articles/PMC1884537/

The V.A. had prescribed him Seroquel, and when he combined that with everything else his pain doctor had prescribed, he overdosed. Even more heartbreaking, their 12-year-old son discovered him clinging to life while Danielle was out of the house.

Greg would go on to survive his first overdose, after spending 16 days on a ventilator, an additional week in the hospital, and four months of rehabilitation.

Danielle practiced "tough love" and kicked him out. He went to live with his parents and entered another in-patient rehab, this time a V.A. facility. Danielle hoped that this would be her husband's wake up call.

"I believed things were going to change. I believed we had finally gotten the fresh start we all deserved."

Danielle believed her prayers had finally been answered. The family was happy again. They were able to spend Thanksgiving and Christmas together.

"I let my guard down. I forgot what addiction was and how it sneaks up on you," said Danielle. "I forgot that every day is a struggle and a choice. I forgot that it doesn't matter where you live, what you do for a living, how much money you have. I forgot that addiction never forgets about you. It's always there, hovering, hunting you down."

Greg was clean for nearly nine months before relapsing.

This time, there wasn't a prescription; there was heroin.

"The 'H' word," Danielle mumbled. "The word I feared. The one word that I used to assuage my own fears, to tell myself that my husband wasn't an addict because he wasn't using heroin."

Her young children would go on to tell her that they had witnessed him shoot up in the kitchen and fall asleep while driving.

During this time, Danielle joined a support group and began going to meetings. She learned how to set boundaries and to no longer enable.

"I reacted quickly," said Danielle. "I kicked him out of the house (again), thinking if I stuck to my guns, he would clean himself up. I mean, he had to, right?"

After Greg expressed to Danielle he no longer wanted to live, Danielle invited him to come over and see his children.

"I didn't recognize the man at my door," said Danielle. "It was like his soul was gone. He had track marks all over his arms, and he was so thin. He looked like hell."

That day, Danielle discovered a letter Greg had written her, expressing how sorry he was for hurting her and their family.

"In the letter, he told me it wasn't my fault that he couldn't just stop," said Danielle. "I just know that once I realized it was never my battle to fight, I found peace. Nothing I could have done or said would have changed the outcome. He had to want it. Just because he didn't, doesn't mean he didn't love us."

Greg then entered rehab for the third time, and though only lasting there two weeks, Greg was clean and staying at a hotel near Danielle's home. He had lined up a job interview and had gone over for dinner every night for two weeks. Danielle and Greg had even gone on a date. Things seemed to be looking up, so Danielle agreed to let Greg watch their kids while she worked one Saturday.

"When I got home, I knew he was high," she said.

Danielle barely spoke to Greg the rest of the evening before she went to bed around 10:00 p.m. Greg was watching a movie with their sons and then was to go back to his hotel.

At 10:30 p.m., Greg entered Danielle's bedroom to see if she needed anything before he left.

At 11:10 p.m. that night, nearly a year to the day of his first overdose, Greg overdosed and died in Danielle's bathroom. Once again, their son discovered him, slumped on the toilet, a needle in the sink that was still running.

What Danielle would go on to uncover in the days and weeks following his death were heart-wrenching.

"There were so many drugs in his hotel room," recounted Danielle. "Credit cards showed he was taking out cash advances. He spent nearly $1,100 on drugs the last week he was alive. The person listed in his phone as his sponsor was actually his drug dealer. It's amazing all the lies you discover after someone dies."

Danielle feels as though she lost a stranger, not the man she married.

"Now, I'm the woman whose husband came for a weekend visit with his children and died in her bathroom," said Danielle. "I forgive him, though. I am at peace because he is no longer struggling and neither am I. I'm free to find myself again. I'm free to be happy. I am free because I am no longer ashamed."

Ten months later, and Danielle and her children are doing well.

"One day I will heal from all of this because if I was strong enough to survive the last few years of my life, I'm strong enough to live again."

"We have a voice, we have a message, we have experience.
We need to speak up and do as much as we can
to *create* change, to *create* hope."

Ada Pasternak
Here's the Story: A Family Disease

Originally Published in the Daily Advertiser on January 28, 2016

MEET MEGAN

As loved ones, it is only natural to beg and plead with the user to "quit" their addiction. It is natural to want to lock them away from the outside world until the drugs leave their system. It is natural to research and call rehabs. And, unfortunately, it is natural for that rehab to alert you that you cannot, in most states, without petitioning the courts, force someone over the age of 18 to admit themselves without their consent.[51]

As loved ones of those who suffer from an addiction, we snap into what I like to call *superhero mode*. We see the damage occurring due to addiction and try to swoop in and save the day.

But those struggling with drug addiction, though in distress, are not damsels.

It is extremely painful to watch someone you love destroy their life, but family members and loved ones cannot control addiction.

And users cannot control the leaps and bounds loved ones will go to in their desperate attempts to "save" them.

Those who suffer from addiction have to save themselves.

Meet Megan, a young woman in recovery.

---

[51] http://www.rehabcenter.net/can-i-get-a-court-order-to-put-my-loved-one-in-rehab/

"It has not always been clear to me that I have a problem," she admitted. "I used to wish I had a hard upbringing to blame things on, a bad childhood, but there isn't a traumatizing backstory to explain why I am the way that I am."

Megan began experimenting with drugs by the age of 14.

Her drug of choice? *Drugs.*

"There was always a reason for why I would do the things I'd do," she explained. "In my mind, I was okay, because I still got the best grades and was still the captain of whatever sports team I was on at the time."

Megan excelled at sports and became a collegiate athlete. It was there, in college and away from her parents, where she truly began to lose control.

She described her first two years of college as "the norm."

"Everyone around me was binge drinking, partying and sleeping around, so at what point would I ever consider it a problem?"

During her third year, Megan was introduced to Adderall. A popular drug with college kids, Megan quickly found herself buying it in bulk.

"What I have learned from being an addict is that even when you have enough of your drug, you never really have enough. It wasn't hard to find on a college campus."

Throughout college campuses in America, there are students with ADHD medication prescriptions who sell pills for cash to fellow students who are not rightfully prescribed the drug.[52]

As a loved one, something you learn is the road to recovery happens in steps, sometimes occurring very far apart, sometimes containing a few steps back for every one step forward, and the moment a user realizes they have a problem is not always the same moment they seek treatment for their addiction.

"The first time I really knew I had a problem was after a 96-hour period of no sleep," Megan told me. "I had a bad drug reaction that led to being in a boot for almost two months. After doing my own research, I realized my body was going through a drug overdose."

Staying up four days straight on nothing but drugs had its repercussions, but it still was not enough for Megan to stop using.

Her junior year was a blur, and after being a "no show" to one too many practices, Megan had to say goodbye to her collegiate career. A lifelong passion of hers became a causality of her addictions.

She began her senior year of college, fell back into heavy drinking, and in April of that year, woke up in jail, scared, still drunk, and cold.

"I knew I couldn't keep living my life this way," Megan told me, and I smiled in relief.

---

[52] http://www.attn.com/stories/3075/college-drug-deals

I imagine anyone reading this story is thinking, as I did, that this was Megan's "wake-up call" and she sought help. Every user has a "rock bottom," but, unfortunately, this wasn't Megan's. Though she stopped abusing prescription drugs, her drinking continued.

Why did someone like Megan - who upheld high grades, was a star athlete, and came from a loving home - fall into the world of addiction?

She is still not sure. No one leads a perfect life, and she said she held onto pain, and didn't deal with it in a healthy manner.

"I was running away from all of the things that would inevitably catch up to me," she said.

In the recovery world, the term "rock bottom" is used to describe a point in the life of a person when they are finally willing to seek help and stop denying their problem.[53]

Megan hit her rock bottom two years and four months after she woke up alone in jail.

"I was tired of my life, and the way I had been living it. Always loving the wrong people, making terrible judgment calls, and ultimately, not being the person I was supposed to be," she expressed. "I was no longer happy, and during my final blackout, I thought I had found the solution."

She attempted to take her own life.

---

[53] http://www.recovery.org/forums/discussion/92/what-does-rock-bottom-mean

Megan spent the next 48 hours in the hospital.

She describes this as the wake-up call she almost didn't wake up from.

"I was given a second chance, and I was determined to make the most of it."

And she has.

"Deciding to be sober was the easiest decision of my life. Actually living sober is the hardest."

Recovery has opened her eyes to a world she wasn't really a part of before.

"I was merely just existing," she said. "Now I feel as though I am involved. I am able to rebuild relationships, and mend the pain I have caused. I am able to forgive myself. I have a purpose now, a reason to keep moving forward."

Recovery most definitely saved Megan's life. Though she recognized she had a problem years before, and despite her parents' efforts in trying to save her, the willpower and ultimate decision to find help had to come from within herself. Her coach couldn't save her. Her friends couldn't save her. Her own parents couldn't save her.

She had to save herself.

This is a harsh reality most loved ones have a problem accepting because it renders us helpless. It could be days, weeks, months, or even years before someone with Substance Use Disorder will truly want to take the steps toward recovery.

And once in recovery, they must make the decision every single day to remain in recovery. For some families, these moments never come, and funerals are planned.

As loved ones, all we can do is help them and encourage them to save themselves. If they're willing to do the work that follows, recovery is possible.

"My sobriety is my favorite thing about me," Megan affirmed. "I am strong enough to overcome the demons that controlled me for so long."

"Recovery means that I have finally shown up for my life," she responded, poignantly.

And her message for anyone reading this who is battling addiction?

"I hope you know you are capable of saving yourself, too."

2017 Update:

I spoke with Megan again on November 20, 2016, when she was one year, three months, and 10 days sober.

"So much has happened in the last 468 days, and I am happy to report that I am still surviving this life with a sober mind, and a healing heart," said Megan. "Since we have last spoken, I have been promoted in my job, I have started my own website, I have learned how to balance a healthy lifestyle,

I have formed a strong support group, I have started to mend all of the damage I caused with those who are closest to me, I have learned how to accept who I am, and I have begun the long journey of loving myself."

"Every single day is a challenge, and every single morning, I remind myself, 'at least you are still alive,'" admitted Megan.

"I look back on the day where I almost ended it all, and I thank whoever was looking over me that night, because I was granted a second chance, and not everyone is that lucky."

Megan has recently decided to move out of her parents' home and to a new city, a dream of hers.

"Living with my parents has allowed me to mend a lot of the damage I have caused with my family, and it has given them more peace of mind knowing that I am doing what I can to be as healthy as I can," said Megan. "I know I have broken that trust, and every day is a chance for me to prove myself to them. I am patient with them, and I make sure to look at things through their perspective, because although I may have accepted what I did, I can't expect that to be so easily accepted by those who don't understand it."

If she has learned anything in the time that she's been sober, it's that we are all even more capable than we ever believed.

"It is usually just ourselves that are in the way of our own growth. We all have a story to share, and you can't judge people based on things that you have never experienced," she said. "I think it's important that we learn to be open minded. Give people a chance no matter what, and allow them to have their own beliefs without forcing what we believe down their throats. I have met so many people carrying a weight that I am happy to not be burdened with, and I have met some of the kindest people that have been dealt some of life's cruelest cards."

Throughout her recovery, Megan has "finally" gotten her priorities in order.

"I may not know what I want to do in this life, but I know who I want to be in this life, and I make sure to strive to be that person every single day. The project of YOU is never over, and what a cool thing it is to know that you can change your life whenever you choose."

Get in touch with Megan:

www.instagram.com/in.my.own.words
www.healinghopefuls.com

Originally Published on the Huffington Post on October 31, 2016

MEET ANNIE

Annie Highwater was introduced to addiction when she was just a young girl. For most of her life, she's known all too well of the tight and quick grasp addiction can have on someone she loves. After an automobile accident, Highwater's mother became addicted to prescription pills; but this story is not about her mother, it's about Highwater's son, Elliot.

"I have always been aware of addiction by virtue of being born into a home affected by it," said Highwater, a self-proclaimed long distance runner and health and wellness advocate. "So, after my son suffered a sport's injury, and was prescribed pills, I watched for signs of dependency."

Unfortunately, all signs of addiction were there, and at just 17-years-old, Highwater's son, a rising star athlete, began abusing prescription opiate pills.

A 2013 study published in the American Journal of Public Health found that adolescent athletes are 50% more likely to abuse painkillers.[54]

The Centers for Disease Control and Prevention hasn't tracked addiction among athletes but says the young adult age group (18-25) has been hit hard, with heroin use more than doubling in the last decade.[55]

---

[54] https://www.ncbi.nlm.nih.gov/pmc/articles/PMC3625478/

[55] https://www.cdc.gov/vitalsigns/heroin/

"Discovering my child was addicted to drugs was like hearing the word 'war,'" said the doting mother. "War was declared against my child, against me, against our home, and definitely against our future. It dropped me to my knees."

Over the course of the next six years, Highwater's family witnessed Elliot's painful descent into the dark world of opiate addiction. The life her family had once known, was changed forever.

"The shame of addiction was isolating and overwhelming," said Highwater. "I felt that we were less than citizens, marked as ruined. Addiction wasn't in the public eye then, as much as it is now. There were some insulting comments, as if we somehow caused or deserved it."

Highwater recalled one parent, the father of a boy who attended school and church with Elliot and also played on baseball and football teams with her son. He told Highwater that his son would never become involved with prescription pills, like Elliot. He said he felt it might have something to do with Elliot's father and Highwater being divorced. He suggested Highwater remarry. He reminded her that *his* son was raised in a two-parent household.

Highwater considers the battle her family endured a success story.

"As a mother, I took my son's dependency on as the fight of my life," expressed Highwater. "Today we are both in recovery; myself as his non-enabling, co-dependent parent. My son is three years into his own path of recovery and sobriety. We are a success story versus a life of misery, defeat, and victim-hood."

Highwater understands the reality of relapse, and chooses not to focus on her son's sobriety date, but enjoys each day as it comes. Highwater will never forget the pain, fear, and anxiety that becomes the "new normal" when one is a parent to a child in active opiate addiction, so she took everything she learned and felt during this life-or-death journey with Elliot and wrote a book. Highwater is actually her penname.

Her memoir, *Unhooked*, chronicles her journey. The memoir was released in October 2016, topping many Amazon charts, and debuted as the #1 Hot New Release in the category of Parent & Child Adult Relationships. The book is published by Six Degrees Publishing Group[56] and is available in paperback and Kindle formats.

"I wrote the book because I wanted to give something helpful to families affected by addiction, particularly mothers like me," explained Highwater. "I had a hard time finding books about an addicted person's family members who are struggling and bewildered. I didn't find much literature available that spoke directly to what I was going through and how terrible I was feeling. I didn't know where to turn, what to do, or what not to do, in the first year."

Not wanting another family member to feel as lost as she once felt, Highwater put this book together as a resource that would inform and empower families where addiction is present.

---

[56] http://www.sixdegreespublishing.com/

"I want other mothers to know you can get through it. As long as there's breath, there's hope," said the mother-turned-author. "We are a family recovering. An addict can recover. A family can recover. I hope my story opens up conversations about addiction within families."

Highwater urges families going through this to become educated on the worlds of addiction and recovery, from becoming familiar with state laws to learning about the effects of different drugs. With so many support groups becoming available to families, she also suggests families build a safe support team, join a group, or find a meeting like Nar-Anon. Lastly, Highwater insists families follow a recovery plan of their own.

"You never know what despair someone is burdened with as you encounter them on the mundane avenues of daily life," reads the final lines of *Unhooked*. "Show kindness, always, because to quote Ram Dass: 'We are all just walking each other home.'"

As the country struggles to address the issues of the rampant epidemic of opiate abuse and addiction, this story is especially relevant in helping us all understand the personal challenges facing parents and family members and how family dynamics both help and hinder the recovery process.

Unhooked is available for purchase on Amazon.

Keep up with Highwater and Unhooked on Facebook:

www.facebook.com/AnnieUnhooked

Originally Published on the Huffington Post on August 10, 2016

MEET JESSE AND HEROES RISING

Our nation is facing the worst drug epidemic in history.[57] That is a fact. Parents are burying their children every day. That is a fact. In response, individuals around the country are fighting back.

Jesse Heffernan is a Certified Recovery Coach. He is a creative, imaginative, forward-thinking, advocate. He is also in recovery.

"I pretty much used whatever I could get my hands on," admitted Heffernan. "Crack was the 'bottoming out' substance in the end, though."

Now, 15 years clean, Heffernan is part of an innovative project that will create meaningful, constructive dialogue about the opioid epidemic in a way that has yet to be explored: through superheroes.

Heroes Rising is a short film produced by Wega Arts, a non-profit organization based in Wisconsin. The film combines comic book style graphics, special effects, and live action. If that was not enough to set it apart, high school students have been working alongside the professional filmmakers as both cast and crew to create this short film.

---

[57] http://www.pbs.org/wgbh/frontline/article/how-bad-is-the-opioid-epidemic/

Heroes Rising is about a high school quarter back, Caleb, who is offered OxyContin. By the time we meet our protagonist, many of his friends are already in the throes of heroin addiction.

Caleb transforms into Captain Solar and, along with his team, the Helios Corps, begins to fight the heroin epidemic.

The movie's official website explains that the theme of the film explores prevention and recovery efforts from facing the facts, to fighting for change, and aims to motivate the youth to view life as a process requiring conviction, courage, and positive actions.[58]

According to Heffernan, a big comic book fan, this project is not only a creative, youthful way to approach the epidemic, but a necessary one. Nationwide resources do not begin to match the problem at hand.

"We need to create more avenues, more ways to have conversations about heroin, opiates, and recovery," said Heffernan.

Heffernan acts as a consultant on the film, from a recovery perspective, and will lead discussions surrounding the film.

"*Heroes Rising* is unique," said Heffernan. "Superheroes are confronting the heroin epidemic. It incorporates comic book and hip-hop elements and stars teenagers. It will resonate with multiple generations and demographics."

---

[58] http://heroesrisingmovie.com/

It is the hope of all those involved with this film that *Heroes Rising* becomes a heavily utilized educational tool in communities and in school districts. They hope to see this movie woven into school curriculums, shown at recovery festivals, and transformed into books.

"Anyone battling addiction is worth it," said Heffernan. "They are worth all the work, all the conversations and interventions."

The majority of the individuals putting in "the work" are the loved ones and those in recovery. Having been on both sides of this grim battle, Heffernan knows how important support systems are first hand.

"It took 101 chances for me to finally get into long-term recovery," expressed Heffernan. "I am eternally grateful no one gave up on me on the 100th chance."

Filming of *Heroes Rising* wrapped in July 2016 and is now in post-production. The film, along with an original soundtrack, will be available nationwide.

2017 Update:

Since the publication of the article in August, the director and producer of the film are still in post-production. Jesse was appointed to the WI Governor's Task Force on Heroin and Opiates.

In December of 2016, Jesse had the chance to present on recovery initiatives in his state and on a pilot project called Recovery Corps.

"Being appointed by the Governor to help develop solutions to the heroin epidemic has been a humbling and empowering experience as a person in long-term recovery," he told me.

Jesse also began a new position as the Director of the Iris Place Peer Run Respite, whose mission is to provide a safe and welcoming environment for individuals who are experiencing emotional distress or crisis. Iris is open every single day of the year, around the clock, and is staffed by a team of nine "peer companions" who are trained to provide support, connect guests to community resources, and support guests as they develop their recovery plans.[59]

Jesse celebrated 16 years in recovery on January 21, 2017.

"The weeks and days leading up to it are always a time of reflection and gratitude for the journey," he noted.

Keep up with Jesse and Helios Recovery:

www.heliosrecovery.com

---

[59] https://www.dhs.wisconsin.gov/library/prririsplace.htm

Originally Published in the Daily Advertiser on February 11, 2016

MEET MELISSA

Though addiction is affecting countless families, the phone calls and conversations on our doorsteps are all different. Different dates, times, durations, reasons, and outcomes.

Melissa's phone call came on March 16, 2012, when she was on a business trip, a plane ride away from her home.

"One of my younger brothers called me saying to get to the hospital. Our brother had been shot ... in the head," she recalled. "At the time of the call, they were running tests to see if he was still alive or not."

The next few hours were the worst of Melissa's entire life. She was hours away from home and had to depend on the airline's schedules to reunite her with her family.

"Have you ever had to drive over an hour, in traffic, in a city you did not know at all, all while trying to remember to breathe?" she asked me, rhetorically. "I don't remember going through security. I know I scared the gate attendant when I hysterically asked if I could get on the plane because my brother had just been shot in the head."

She got on the plane.

Melissa's brother had been addicted to meth for years, and their relationship had been rocky, to say the least, and at times, violent. Melissa told me he chased her around the house with a machete when she was 16, and when she was 17, he threatened to kill her. She believed him, so she moved out.

He'd been in and out of jail for the drugs and the crimes he'd commit to support this habit. The last time she saw her brother before the phone call was in January 2012 at her niece's birthday party.

"With tears in his eyes and his entire body shaking, he told me he thought about doing meth every minute of every day," Melissa said. "But he was committed to staying clean and sober and away from his friends for the next year. We took a picture together that day."

That picture was the one Melissa's family used on his memorial card. Her brother died in the hospital.

"I loved my brother very much. I felt so much heartache, sadness, and guilt after he passed," Melissa admitted. "Growing up I called him a 'loser,' and probably much worse, for the choices he made. He used to make me so mad."

Many loved ones battle with guilt after losing someone. They wonder if they could have done more. They regret things they may have said out of anger. They wish for second chances, more pictures, and more time.

As much as this tragedy altered Melissa's life forever, addiction was not done with her. Addiction is not lightning; it can, and will, strike the same family twice.

Fast forward a couple of years later, and Melissa received another phone call.

She learned her youngest brother had developed a heroin addiction.

He had a bad back, and instead of having surgery, his doctor put him on Percocet and OxyContin.

Heroin addicts aren't born every day; they are manufactured.

Though there is some predisposition for addiction, addiction has to be perpetuated, and many argue that "big pharma" is a major influencer.[60]

Those pills prescribed to Melissa's younger brother are, for lack of better terms, legal heroin, sometimes selling for five times more on the street than a bag of heroin. It is a common statistic that four out of five people who become addicted to heroin first experiment with pills.[61]

Melissa's story echoes these facts.

"When he no longer had insurance and was not able to get his prescription filled, he tried heroin."

He was homeless for a while and has been incarcerated since 2015.

---

[60]http://www.huffingtonpost.com/alex-lawson/no-accident-deadly-greed_b_9031038.html

[61]http://www.asam.org/docs/default-source/advocacy/opioid-addiction-disease-facts-figures.pdf

Unlike last time, Melissa did not feel guilt or sadness; she got angry.

"I was angry that he was putting our family through this. Anger is a higher, more spiritual vibration than depression and sadness. We take action when we get angry."

And that's what she did. Melissa is a trained relationship coach, applied her skills to the addiction universe and created Oak Creek Wellness (www.oakcreekwellness.com), a production company committed to creating inspirational content.

Melissa does not believe her heartache, at the hands of addiction, is any different from any other heartache.

"We all have heartache in our lives," Melissa empathized. "Those heartbreaks do not define us; it's what we do as a result of experiencing them that defines us."

Within Oak Creek Wellness, Melissa founded the Addiction Support Podcast, addiction support for family and friends. She also kicked off the 60 Seconds of Solitude Podcast.

"It's a quick, easy, daily meditation to support people in living in the now," she explained.

"Depression comes in when we are focused on the past. Anxiety comes in when we are worried about the future. Peace, power, and happiness come when we can live in the moment."

I asked her what she hopes people take away from her mission and story.

"I want my contribution to be one that lifts and inspires others," she answered.

Then she told me something about the brother she lost in March 2012 that sent chills up my spine.

"My brother was an organ donor. He was able to prolong the life of five other people," she smiled. "You see, it does not matter who you are or what you've done; it is never too late to leave the world a better place than you found it."

2017 Update:

Melissa is now a contributing author in *A Day in My Head* by Aron Bennett.[62] *A Day in My Head* is a compilation of stories from people who both have mental illness and who have mental illness in their family. In the book, she shares a recent story of her youngest brother whose behavior led her to believe he might be dead.

She is pitching a television show that will help end the stigma and show the recovery process as part of a normal human journey.

"We want to highlight the fact that addiction is a family disease and we all need help to get through it," said Melissa.

---

[62] https://www.amazon.com/Day-My-Head-Aron-Bennett/dp/178382316X

Melissa is also putting together an e-Course that will help people deal with the initial pain, denial, and heartbreak of realizing their family member suffers from addiction.

"It's a bridge for people who aren't ready to admit to others and aren't quite ready for therapy or a support group," explained Melissa.

Contact Melissa:

www.AddictionSupportPodcast.com

Originally Published in the Daily Advertiser on April 12, 2016

MEET CHRISTINA

Christina turned 23 on March 18, 2016.

Her phone rang, as many phones do on birthdays, but when Christina answered, the person on the other end told her that her mother overdosed and died. She was only 49-years-old.

I spoke with Christina three weeks later.

"As if the death of my mother isn't heartbreaking enough," Christina said. "Now I have to be reminded of the worst day of my entire life on the day my life actually began."

Christina knew her mother "wasn't right" from a very early age. She recalls not even being a teenager and noticing her mother's behavior and seeing the symptoms of long-term drug abuse like bruised arms and pinhole pupils. She just didn't know what to call it yet.

By her freshman year of high school in 2007, Christina's father finally told her that her mother was addicted to heroin. This was right before her mother left for rehab.

"I knew heroin was a bad drug, but that's all I knew," Christina admitted. "I didn't know how much it could change a person. I didn't know addiction was a treatable, but incurable, disease."

Immediately following this discovery, Christina began educating herself about drug addiction.

"All I wanted to do was understand, but educating yourself does not create an understanding of addiction. Experience does."

After only speaking with Christina a little while, I could see that though she is young, her life experiences due to addiction have made her very insightful.

I am impressed with her wealth of knowledge on this topic but know how much innocence has been lost in the process. An innocence she will never get back. Unfortunately, Christina experienced the heartbreaking journey many loved ones know all too well.

Christina's mother battled heroin addiction for almost 30 years, cycling between active addiction and recovery.

Drug overdoses are the leading cause of accidental deaths in the US, with 47,055 lethal drug overdoses in 2014. Opioid addiction is driving this epidemic, with 18,893 overdose deaths.[63]

Those battling addictions are not any less human than those who aren't. They are connected to others; they have families, romantic relationships, children, friends, co-workers, and neighbors.

Sadly, when someone overdoses and dies, the whispers usually pass it off simply.

"He lived like an addict,
he died like one too."

---

[63]http://www.asam.org/docs/default-source/advocacy/opioid-addiction-disease-facts-figures.pdf

"He was just a drug addict."

That simplification isn't accurate and is unfair to the grieving loved ones. No one is "just a drug addict." The perception of addiction manages to sum up a complex human being into something one-dimensional. When someone dies, regardless of the reason, it means their heart stopped beating, blood stopped flowing, a life ended. It means a person someone loved took their last breath.

They leave people behind.

Some of the most vulnerable causalities are children, like Christina, who are suddenly without a parent.

In the last four years, Christina lost both of her parents. Her father passed away in 2012 from a liver disease. Christina believes she lost her mother years before she ever died.

"When I lost my dad, I lost my mom, too," Christina explained. "She wasn't my mother anymore, but my addict."

This was Christina's heartbreaking way of telling me her mother had relapsed after the loss of her husband.

"I suddenly wasn't her daughter anymore, but her mother," Christina started. "I had to constantly ask her where she was, who she was with, when she'd be coming home. I had to make sure bills were paid. I even gained the authority to kick her out of her own house."

Christina's tale is nothing less than tragic, but familiar.

Christina's story is unique, as every person's story is, but the underlining issue that tethers Christina to so many other loved ones is this: heroin is poison, and it is killing the people we love in rapid succession.

Christina hopes that other children living in homes riddled with addiction remember that their parents love them, but they are sick, and because of that, the drugs come first.

"That's part of their disease," she said, matter-of-factly. It was then that I saw there was true acceptance in her eyes. There was no anger, no resentment.

"Drugs took hold of her and took her from me. It was nothing I did. So, at some point, acceptance is the goal. It took me six years, but I finally made it to acceptance, and I am glad I did," Christina told me. "My mother has my heart and though it has been broken beyond repair, I know she doesn't have to fight this battle anymore, and neither does my family."

Christina did have a few years with her mother when she was clean. She loved her more than anyone else in the world. And now, just a few short weeks since losing her, she has something to say to her mother.

"This story is for you, Mom, because I want you to know that I understand addiction now. I love you unconditionally, my mother and my addict."

2017 Update:

It has been approximately 10 months since Christina's mother's passing.

"My family and I have been grieving together, but saying it has been easy would be a lie," said Christina. "For me personally, the death of my mother has been extremely hard to deal with when thinking about it, so I don't. I can easily distract myself with work, school, and friends which aren't necessarily healthy ways to grieve, but that's how I have been coping."

Since her mother's passing, she has been promoted to a case manager at a women's residential program, working with women who are recovering from Substance Use Disorder.

"Working in the field of substance abuse has not only been rewarding and challenging, but has helped me understand the disease of addiction better, in which I understand my mom better, even though she is no longer here," said Christina.

"The opioid epidemic of today, and the drastic increase in overdose deaths has created a substantial amount of fear, not only in the public, but in my clients who are in recovery."

Narcan training has been a requirement for not only the staff at Christina's place of employment, but for the clients, as well.

"To me, this disease is so real, and it should appear that way to the public, too. Drug awareness of this opioid epidemic is a topic that needs to be discussed more, in schools, in the news, and especially on social media," stressed Christina.

"Coming together as a community to bring awareness is the first step in the right direction to manage this epidemic because people are dying and families are suffering, including my own," she went on to say.

Ten months later and Christina continues to grieve.

"I have managed to create the best life for myself because that is what my parents would have wanted for me," said Christina. "I have promised myself to actively help clients stay motivated toward recovery and be a voice for families who are suffering, to let them know they're not alone and it is possible to find peace."

Wish Christina a "Happy Birthday" on Facebook:

www.facebook.com/christina.devlin.731

Originally Published on the Huffington Post on November 21, 2016

MEET ANTHONY AND RISE TOGETHER

As the end of 2016 nears, closing with it one of the deadliest years in drug-related deaths in recent history[64], many events and programs at schools are trying their hardest to bring attention back to the drug prevention model.

According to an article on CNN, though children may receive some anti-drug messaging through programs, like D.A.R.E., it is just not enough as research has shown that program has had no real impact on the rate of drug use.[65]

In that same article, drug awareness advocates stated that what our youth needs is prevention-education during their teenage years when their brains are not yet fully developed to assess risk. More so, the teenage years are when the presence and opportunity to use drugs increases.

Anthony Alvarado is a co-founder of Rise Together, a grass roots organization rising to the challenge and committed to helping youth stand up and speak out on issues plaguing their generation; like drugs and alcohol.

---

[64]http://www.cnn.com/2016/09/23/health/heroin-opioid-drug-overdose-deaths-visual-guide/

[65] http://www.cnn.com/2016/01/15/health/addiction-schools-education-prevention/

In the last three years, Rise Together has traveled over 100,000 miles, partnered with over 150 schools, presented over 400 times, and has educated over 120,000 students. Rise Together primarily engages middle schools, high schools, colleges, and other public settings by providing a variety of speaking engagements, special events, public panels, and workshops.

"As a recovery advocacy group we have a passion for prevention, education, and community outreach," said Alvarado, of the organization he created with Douglas Darby and Nadine Machkovech. "Rise Together has been actively involved in the community since September 2013. Today, Rise Together is led by a team of dedicated professionals from a diverse background of educations, professions, and skill sets."

Rise Together provides a strategic amount of services that not only bring value to students but also to parents, businesses, and the community. The mission of Rise Together is to help students stand up for what they believe in, and encourage them to become the advocates of change their communities so desperately need.

"Our school-speaking program is also not just 'one and done' as we are now launching a student-led and life skills curriculum, called *The RAISE Project*, in the spring of 2017," added Alvarado. "This will serve as a catalyst to the cultural change that needs to take place to support those suffering from an addiction and mental illness, or to those who are finding it difficult to cope with life challenges."

Acting as an extension of their physical presence, Rise Together also extends education and awareness opportunities through the Rise & Grind Radio Podcast, which is available on iTunes and Rise Together's website.

Alvarado himself is in long-term recovery. After using drugs for over 10 years, Alvarado began his recovery journey eight years ago.

"Addiction truly brought me to the darkest places I have ever traveled. Already, by the young age of 24, I felt physically, mentally, emotionally, and spiritually broken. It was at that point, eight years ago, that I truly felt like death was the only way out of addiction," recalled Alvarado. "I was broken, and all I wanted was for the shame and guilt to go away. Thankfully, at one of my lowest points, my children helped remind me that life is worth living."

Not wanting his children to grow up in a world where drug use runs rampant, Alvarado along with his business partners, founded Rise Together.

"As a father of two beautiful children, I can't just stand there, doing nothing, while our country faces a social crisis," said Alvarado. "The public services we provide are just some examples of what needs to take place to eliminate the social stigma around addiction and mental health. Prevention, education, and awareness are indeed key."

Rise Together is making a measurable difference in the world. Since 2014, Rise Together has surveyed nearly 7,000 students across 47 counties in Alvarado's home state of Wisconsin, and have found that an overwhelming amount of young people are affected by significant trauma, large amounts of stress, substance use disorders, self-harm, suicidal tendencies, and other mental and behavioral health conditions.[66]

---

[66] http://skywoodrecovery.com/student-snapshot-middle-school-and-high-school-students-on-substance-use/

"We are successfully helping to identify the pulse of our young people; especially teens. While we are educating through storytelling, we are also able to perform research throughout the communities we visit," explained Alvarado. "This not only allows us to discover key findings of teen substance use but also discover viable solutions."

For example, 80% of the students surveyed indicated that they are less likely to use drugs and alcohol after seeing a Rise Together presentation.

Additionally, students have identified a need for more school prevention and intervention and education strategies to help combat the drug epidemic our country is facing.

In other words, our youth is aware of the problems their communities face, and they want to learn more, they want to address it, and they even want to step up and get involved to help make changes.

"Addiction is a family disease that impacts entire homes while threatening the health and well-being of the entire family," said Alvarado, whose own father was recently hospitalized due to addiction. "We must still learn to show that we love them unconditionally and offer our consistent support. We must also remember that we cannot forget to take care of ourselves. If we don't take of ourselves, we can't take care of others. This is why it is crucial for you to find additional support and resources."

2017 Update:

According to Rise Together's official newsletter, in 2016 Rise Together traveled to five different states, educated 1,000's of students, grew as a business, strengthened their focus, and developed a stronger purpose, vision, and mission.

2017 holds very exciting developments for Rise Together such as:

- The Rise Together Advisory Board
- New strategic partnerships
- New products & services
- Rise & Grind Recovery Radio will go "worldwide"

"And we, of course, are going back on the Rise Together Educational School-Speaking Tour to empower students to become resilient leaders from fifth grade all the way up through college," noted the newsletter.

Help support Rise Together and keep up with them on social media!

www.gofundme.com/help-prevent-addiction-save-lives
www.weallrisetogether.org/
www.instagram.com/risetogether_official/
www.facebook.com/weallrisetogether

MEET MARV AND ONE REP AT A TIME

Marv is 30 and lives in Southern California. A believer in exercise, he owns and manages a gym focused exclusively on people in recovery. Recently, Marv launched a blog that links together all aspects of fitness into the challenges faced by those in recovery.

Up until three years ago, Marv was slowly killing himself with alcohol, drugs, and performance enhancers.

Identity issues, major surgeries, battles with Body Dysmorphia, and depression triggered Marv's drug seeking behavior and led him down the very isolated and dangerous path far too many find themselves. Before even graduating high school, Marv was using hard drugs and drinking regularly.

"I remember my first drunk, it was a life-changing moment," recalled Marv. "All of a sudden my feelings of inadequacy and self-doubt vanished. I became smarter, sexier, more confident, able to talk to girls easily, you name it. I found drugs shortly after and within a year things progressed to out of control proportions."

Using drugs and alcohol as escape mechanisms quickly took control of his life and resulted in failing out of college his first year and enrolling in a place he never saw himself: an outpatient treatment program.

"At 19, I was nowhere near ready to honestly admit I was an alcoholic and addict," confessed Marv.

In the few years following the program, he did manage to get off hard drugs and began only drinking on weekends, before he found himself using and drinking all day, every day again.

After enrolling in college again, Marv was introduced to exercise, weight lifting in particular, and was diagnosed with body dysmorphic disorder (BDD).[67]

"I was still massively insecure in my early twenties and was trying to fill a void inside myself. I decided I wanted the 'perfect body,'" said Marv. "Within two years of lifting my first weight, I made the uninformed and uneducated decision to hop on athletic drugs as I had grown too impatient with my results."

During this time, Marv was studying earn a Bachelor's Degree in Kinesiology. Every day, while he was destroying his own body with substances and alcohol, he was learning how to repair and improve the human body.

The irony of this was not lost on Marv.

"I remember days I literally had my loaded steroid syringe, bong, glass of whiskey, and bottle of pills all out in front of me to put in my body before riding my bike to class to perform exercise physiology experiments in a lab," said Marv.

Even though Marv partied and poisoned himself daily, he managed to graduate college with a Bachelor of Science Degree in Exercise Science.

---

[67]http://www.mayoclinic.org/diseases-conditions/body-dysmorphic-disorder/home/ovc-20200935

His body and mind began to react dangerously to all the toxins, and in 2011, his body began to shut down. He lost nearly 70 pounds in nine months and found himself admitted to a unit of a psych ward and then his first inpatient treatment center.

"The psych ward should have been enough for me. The treatment program should have been enough to convince me I was a drug addict and alcoholic in desperate need of some sort of a recovery program," reflected Marv. "Literally dragging myself down the hallway to my parents' room at three in the morning, withdrawing and in the midst of a panic attack should have been my bottom, but I wasn't yet ready to put down the shovel."

So, Marv kept digging himself deeper and deeper, becoming a master manipulator and liar to those who cared most about him. He was once again portraying himself outwardly as someone he was not: someone who had hit bottom and was willing to go to any lengths to maintain sobriety.

"I did very little to make my recovery a reality," admitted Marv. "Unfortunately there is not a way to translate the pain and hurt families feel into making the user want to get clean and sober. Unless someone wants recovery, it is going to be an uphill struggle. Recovery is not for everyone who needs it; it is for those who want it."

Marv did not work 12-steps, did not get a sponsor, and did not really work on himself after treatment. Before long, he was relapsing in secret, celebrating his sobriety with friends, family, and in meetings, but still using. Marv began experiencing suicidal thoughts and staged a public relapse as a cry for help.

Even still, shame and denial held Marv back, once again, from recovery.

"I bounced in and out of the rooms for the next year or so. During this time, I did things that are of ill-approach, things that put black spots onto my soul, to say the least," said Marv. "Finally on June 22, 2013, I hit my bottom, I hit my point of surrender."

Truly ready to heal and recover, Marv quit his job as an insurance agent, moved out of his house, put all of his possessions in storage, and checked into a very intensive four-month behavior modification program.

"It took me about a month of being in that facility before I was able to get honest, let down the charade I was still stupidly portraying, and truly start working on myself," said Marv. "I am very grateful for that facility and all it provided me. I learned more about myself in those four short months than the 27 years combined previously. I go back at least twice a month carrying H&I panels to this day in an effort to give back."

After transitioning out of that facility, Marv began serious work of the 12-steps and moved into a sober living house, where he remained for over two years, and found work again. Marv worked all 12-steps within his first year of sobriety and has changed his relationship with exercise.

Today, exercise has become a spiritual endeavor for Marv, and he is proud to announce he has restored a healthy balance to his life that allows him to work on improving his physical, mental, emotional, and spiritual well-being.

"Those black spots on my soul slowly started to lessen and vanish," expressed Marv. "Something resembling self-esteem and self-worth started to surface."

This past year has been a true test of his recovery. His mother died suddenly and his girlfriend was diagnosed with breast cancer. Thankfully, his girlfriend is now in remission after receiving treatment.

During heartbreaking moments in life, relapse is very possible, as many view using as their only way to cope.[68] Marv did not return to old behaviors.

In the last year, Marv discovered his own way to give back to the rooms that gave him back his life, by opening his gym and blogging about how exercise and health can and should be beneficial and something that does not control, but improves, your life.

"I cannot begin to describe what it means to be able to look myself in the eyes in a mirror and recognize the man looking back," said Marv. "Getting clean and sober has the potential to be the single greatest thing I have ever done. I say 'potential' because, at any given minute, I can choose to give it away. If this ever happens I could not be mad at the disease of addiction, I could not be mad at whatever event or person I would falsely use to blame for my relapse. I could only be mad at myself because I know exactly what I need to do every single day to protect and improve my recovery."

Marv knows that even as people read this story about how he turned his life around, there are people out there who are entering recovery programs, or sadly, using and dying.

---

[68]http://www.huffingtonpost.com/dr-howard-samuels/relapse-prevention_b_3326444.html

"If you are battling an addiction, you are not an evil person who needs to get righteous, you are a sick person who needs to get better," stressed Marv. "That is a huge distinction. No matter what your head is telling you, you deserve to live a great life."

2017 Update:

"I am still clean and sober, still involved in 12-step fellowships, still training people in recovery, still working on building my blog and online presence," Marv told me. "I am very blessed and very happy that I have found my life's mission!"

Keep up with Marv and One Rep at a Time:

www.onerepatatime.net
www.facebook.com/onerepatatime
www.twitter.com/onerepatatime

Originally Published on the Huffington Post on August 18, 2016

MEET LAURA

Laura Silverman woke up in New York City, still tired and groggy from the night before. It was the first time she, a resident of Washington D.C., ever visited the City. She wasn't in a comfy hotel bed though; she was in the hospital. For alcohol poisoning. And it wasn't the first time.

"I drank for six years," said Silverman. "At first it was fun, then fun with problems, then just problems. When I was hospitalized that second time and woke up relatively unscathed, it felt like divine intervention or something a little bigger than just me."

After being reunited with her cousin and her belongings, Silverman checked herself into an outpatient program in D.C. through her health insurance provider. This marked the beginning of her journey to recovery. Today, she is nine years sober and the founder of The Sobriety Collective, an online powerhouse that celebrates sobriety and the arts.[69]

"The Sobriety Collective is special because it caters to creatives who are in recovery from substance use disorder, mental illness, or both," said Silverman.

The idea to build a safe place where those in recovery can share their stories with a community that understands hit Silverman as she celebrated her eighth year of sobriety.

---

[69] http://www.thesobrietycollective.com/welcome-home

"I felt an emptiness inside. I wasn't practicing a program, not a formal one, anyway, and I didn't have any sober friends," admitted Silverman. "I desperately wanted to be a part of a community, and so, not knowing what was already out there, I created what I needed at the time."

Silverman, like many other advocates, hopes to show the world that recovery is not only possible, but those in recovery can go on to make positive impacts in their communities, and, the world.

"My vision for the Collective is to have it be a living, breathing community of awesome sober people, making contributions in music, film, writing, fashion, technology, beauty, business, comedy, photography, art, philanthropy, education, you name it," explained Silverman.

Silverman has achieved her goal tens time over, having created the vibrant, active community she imagined over one year ago. The Sobriety Collective has a robust website filled with great, honest information and resources including a blog, a store, a recovery profile section, a podcast, and a page with helpful resources.

The success of the Sobriety Collective is a constant reminder to Silverman just how far she has come since that morning she woke up in the hospital.

"I've definitely had my ups and downs throughout nine years, but I have a strong commitment to living a better life in recovery," said Silverman. "I'm not immune to temptation, but I'm very much in control of my choices and actions. I wouldn't dare trade nine consecutive years of sobriety for a drink or two, or three, or fifteen, or one hundred..."

At her lowest, Silverman was able to successfully springboard herself into recovery. She hopes those battling Substance Use Disorder know they can do the same, and do not have to do it alone.

"Get help. You have a disease that requires treatment, like any other person with any other disease. You are not your addiction," stressed Silverman. "There is hope, and if you can see even just a glimmer of it, take a chance right now. Don't think you'll get chance after chance after chance. Call a professional, lean on family, if you can. The only failure is the failure to do something."

In five years Silverman sees herself traveling the world, spending time with close family and friends, living sober and debt-free, practicing yoga near the ocean, re-learning to play guitar, and helping others achieve their true paths in recovery.

2017 Update:

Since Laura's story was published, she's accepted a position as Community Outreach Coordinator at NorthStar Academy (www.northstaracademy-metrodc.com), a day treatment program with a recovery school environment for bright yet struggling teens. She is excited to use her recovery advocacy in a meaningful way and looks forward to influencing the lives of a new generation.

In April of 2017, The Sobriety Collective will celebrate its second anniversary and, in July, Laura will celebrate 10 years of continuous sobriety. Laura is immensely grateful for the spirited community she has found through the #recoveryfriendlyweb.

Contact Laura:

www.thesobrietycollective.com

MEET SHATTERPROOF

www.shatterproof.org

Shatterproof is a national nonprofit organization dedicated to ending the devastation addiction causes families. Based in New York City, Shatterproof is the first national organization to attack addiction from all perspectives, providing advocacy, family support, and evidence-based resources to anyone affected by this disease.

Shatterproof was founded in 2013 by Gary Mendell. Mendell, a former hotel CEO, sought out to turn the loss of his son, Brian, into hope and created Shatterproof in his honor.

"He was as good a son as anyone could ask for," said Mendell, in a video on Shatterproof's official website.[70] "Through the randomness of biology, genetics, or some other factor, Brian became addicted."

This set the Mendell family on a 10-year journey of rehabs and psychiatrists; a path that would quickly become any parent's worst nightmare.

Brian was clean for a year and five weeks when he wrote a note to his family, expressing his guilt. He apologized to them and wrote he felt terrible for what he had put his family through over the years.

Then, he lit a candle and took his own life, leaving the world feeling ashamed of what he did to his family.

---

[70] https://www.shatterproof.org/

Since its inception, Shatterproof has hosted the largest national event series focused on addiction, The Shatterproof Challenge Rappel, as well as a myriad of other events. Believing growth is never over, the Organization recently relaunched their website in October, filling it to the brim with even more resources about addiction prevention, treatment, and recovery, as well as information on the science of addiction.

Jessica Keefe is the Senior Editor at Shatterproof. Keefe joined the Organization after losing her little brother to an opioid overdose in 2015.

"We aim to spare other families the pain of addiction by reducing the deadly stigma of addiction that keeps people from getting the treatment they need," said Keefe.

According to Keefe, in just over three years, Shatterproof has helped change laws around addiction in 11 states, held numerous successful events, and united thousands of families across the country. Keefe has every confidence they'll only increase these successes as the Organization grows.

"Silence and stigma costs lives. Speak up," Keefe advised.

"What I failed to understand as a parent, was that Brian's chemistry had been changed," Mendell went on to say in the video. "Addiction is a disease. If we can understand that as a society, and show empathy, more people would seek treatment, fewer people would die, and fewer families would be shattered beyond repair. The foundation of change is shifting how the public views addiction. This is my life's work now."

"Addiction is about chemistry, not character," added Mendell.

MEET LAURIE

"To me, they're murders," said the stepfather of Brandon Morris. "They should be tried for murder."[71]

Morris' stepfather was referring to the two drug dealers who failed to call for help as they watched his stepson overdose on May 15, 2015. By the time Morris arrived at the hospital, he was attached to a ventilator, and despite going to extreme measures to lessen brain swelling, it was just too late. Brandon was pronounced dead on May 16, 2015.

"I screamed his name. He was there in the hospital bed and looked so healthy. I just kept thinking, 'this can't be,'" said Morris' mother, Laurie Clemons. "My body was in shock. They told us they tried Narcan on him twice to no avail."

Clemons describes her son as an outgoing, all-American boy who loved to play football and go fishing.

"He was always there for me," Clemons said. "Brandon was a typical Mama's Boy."

His love of sports resulted in injuries that then resulted in prescription pills. Morris became addicted.

"The doctors would prescribe him 30 pills, plus refills. Doctors had no problem prescribing them," recounted Clemons.

---

[71]http://www.13abc.com/content/news/Couple-to-read-letters-at-Millbury-mans-sentencing--387367171.html

"I never expected Brandon would stick a needle in his arm," Clemons added. "We don't want this to happen to anyone else's family. The heartache is just unbearable."

His mother estimates he moved on from pills to heroin in 2014 after his relationship with a woman addicted to heroin ended and he began to ask for money. Eventually, Morris moved back home with his mother and stepfather, no longer being able to hide his addiction. Morris' family began noticing two men meeting him outside the house on a regular basis.

One day in July of 2014, his stepfather found needles in Morris' laundry.

"I was in so much shock, Brandon never liked needles, he hated getting his allergy shots," his mother said.

The day following the discovery, he went to rehab for one week, and then entered an outpatient program and began taking Suboxone.

The two men that would frequent their home turned out to be drug dealers.

"We found out the names of the two men, and we spoke to our police department," said Clemons. "The police department did nothing about it."

After witnessing her son relapse, Clemons practiced "tough love" and asked Morris to move out. For four months, Clemons met with her son to make sure his car had gas, and he had food to eat. During this time, Morris managed to keep his full-time job he had held down for nearly a decade.

In April of 2015, Morris agreed to go back into treatment, this time in Florida. He completed the entire five-week program, returning home on Mother's Day. Clemons now has a tattoo of her son's inscription from his final Mother's Day card.

"Brandon had gained all his weight back from 125 pounds to 155 pounds, and was acting like *my Brandon* again," recounted Clemons, adding that Brandon had decided to return to Florida as soon as he could to avoid the triggers of his old environment, even meeting with his job to see if a transfer was possible.

Clemons later learned that the day he returned home, the two men Clemons had alerted the police to, began texting her son.

"They knew he would be an easy sale and trigger him to use again since Brandon was only clean for five weeks," explained Clemons.

Within five days of being home, Brandon overdosed, was hospitalized, and died.

The day Morris was pronounced dead, Clemons received a call from a woman her son knew.

"She told me she had Brandon's suitcase and belongings and wanted to give them to us," explained Clemons. "I asked how she got them and she told me two men had asked her to give them to us. She said Brandon was dropped off at the outside of the hospital."

Clemons' husband and daughter attained the hospital security tape and were able to identify the drug dealer who dropped her son off as one of the men who sold her son drugs.

"They never called 911 because they both had warrants out for their arrests," said Clemons. "One of them called their own mother, who turned out to be a nurse, but didn't call 911. They just let him die."

This time, when Clemons went after the two drug dealers, the legal system and police listened.

One of the men will serve three years in prison and three years on parole without the opportunity to appeal the sentence.[72]

Until recently, overdoses were treated as accidents. Now, a growing number of law enforcement officials around the country are prosecuting drug dealers for causing heroin overdose deaths.[73]

Gone, but truly not forgotten, Morris' giving spirit has been able to continue. While her son was in the hospital, Clemons learned that he could be considered for organ donation, even though he was an intravenous drug user and died of an overdose.

Doctors were able to match Morris' liver to a 57-year-old grandfather, who happened to be a recovering alcoholic. Within a year of Morris' death, she met the man saved by her son's liver. She now considers the organ recipient and his wife like family.

According to ABC News, the rise of people dying as a result of the nation's opioid epidemic has caused the number of

---

[72] http://www.13abc.com/content/news/Man-involved-in-heroin-death-receives-his-sentence-387522761.html

[73]http://www.drugfree.org/news-service/prosecutors-charging-drug-dealers-in-heroin-overdose-deaths/

organ donations from fatal overdose victims to rise - an unexpected consequence that highlights the nation's excruciating opioid crisis.

According to the United Network for Organ Sharing (UNOS), the nonprofit organization that manages the nation's organ transplant system, in 1994, only 29 donors in the U.S. had died of drug overdoses. Last year, that number climbed to 848.[74]

"The rise in numbers is not due solely to the increase in opioid overdoses. Medical advances have also allowed more organs from drug-intoxicated donors, which were often unusable for transplantation, to save the lives of some people facing long waiting lists," stated the article.

The U.S. Centers for Disease Control and Prevention classifies an organ transplant from an IV drug user as "high risk" because, statistically, it holds a higher risk for HIV and hepatitis B or C. Thus, recipients must specifically consent to receive a donation from a "high risk" donor.[75]

The "risks" have lessened due to new tests that can detect these diseases in a rather short period.[76]

Clemons said she chose to donate her son's organs because she knew the pain of losing her own son and hoped that no other family would have to experience the loss of a child.

---

[74] https://www.unos.org/

[75] https://news.vice.com/article/the-us-drug-overdose-epidemic-has-made-it-easier-to-get-an-organ-transplant

[76] https://www.ncbi.nlm.nih.gov/pmc/articles/PMC3675207/

"Brandon would be happy to know that he saved someone's life," said Clemons. "Even though his life ended in a tragedy, he helped someone live on. Brandon is a hero," said Clemons.

Since losing Brandon, she and her family have dedicated a lot of time advocating for increased awareness of the opioid epidemic and organ donations.[77]

Most recently, Morris' former high school held a "Volley for Life" event. The event was designed to raise organ donor awareness as well as the growing opiate problem plaguing the nation.

"The community needs to be involved in this epidemic. It's the only way we're going to get a handle on this," Clemons said.[78]

The man already charged has pleaded down and has agreed to testify against the other dealer. The second man being charged in the death of Morris is scheduled to be sentenced in March.[79]

[77]http://abcnews.go.com/US/drug-overdose-deaths-drive-increase-number-organ-donations/story?id=42401899

[78]http://www.13abc.com/content/news/Volley-for-Life-honors-Cardinal-Stritch-graduate-who-died-of-an-overdose-393198581.html

[79]http://www.13abc.com/content/news/Couple-to-read-letters-at-Millbury-mans-sentencing--387367171.html

Originally Published in the Daily Advertiser on November 9, 2015

MEET BLU

There is a stigma within our society that those who abuse drugs or alcohol, despite the consequences, are weak or morally failed. A belief users can be identified in a room full of people. A belief users wear their addiction like a scarlet letter. A belief users do not aspire to be anything more than drug addicts.

The reality is, today's drug users don't always fit the stereotype.

Blu battled a three-year addiction to methamphetamine while she was in college, unbeknownst to any of her classmates or professors. Not only that, she graduated from her university in Miami, Florida with honors and a 3.66 GPA, all while fighting her addiction.

Blu had a brutal childhood. Her father was physically and verbally abusive to the entire family - Blu, her mother, and her brother, one time choking Blu for so long, she passed out, only to awaken with his hands still firmly around her neck.

She was in foster care for a year while her parents battled to regain custody. Blu attempted suicide twice as a child, once at age 9, and again at 11.

In hopes to escape her personal Hell and create a "nuclear family" of her own, she married at 16 and had a child one year later. Blu, admittedly, was not ready for all that came along with being a wife and mother. Four years into her marriage, at just 20-years-old, she left her husband and family in search of "freedom."

Depressed and working in the club scene, she soon fell into the world of drugs. First getting hooked on cocaine, she later found a "better high" in snorting, then smoking, crystal meth.

"It starts out small," she told me. "You're happy. You use. You're celebrating. You use. You're sad. You use. You're mad. You use. You have a bad day. You use. You have an alright day. You use. Before you know it, without even realizing, you're using to survive."

Around this time, at 22, she met a man. He was not a drug abuser and had his own successful business. He even gave her a job working for him.

He had no idea Blu was addicted to drugs.

Blu was not ready to face her addiction and get the help she needed. She began to steal to support her habit, writing checks from her boyfriend's company, as she had access to all his bank accounts and financial records.

Unlike the stereotypes, Blu still desired a life outside the drug world. She had dreams. She had goals. She wanted to reconnect with her son, who was quickly growing up. Due to her tough childhood, time in foster care, and the different therapists she had to see because of her experiences, Blu knew she wanted to help people.

She decided to enroll in college and pursue a degree in psychology, with aspirations to become a drug counselor. Yet, she was still in the midst of addiction herself.

She used crystal meth every single day for three years, staying up days at a time, and no one had a clue. She still showed up to her classes, aced her tests, and participated actively in class discussions.

"I was battling this dark secret no one knew about. And if they had suspicions, they didn't know how deep my addiction went."

By this time, Blu needed the drug to function, or she would spiral into horrible withdrawal. However, as she immersed herself in her studies, she began to learn exactly what she was doing to herself, physically and mentally. Everything she was reading, unknown to others, she was experiencing in real life due to her addiction. Through education, she was able to learn about the psychological damage her father caused and the depression that stemmed from her upbringing. She quickly realized she was self-medicating.

She called this an epiphany, and she knew at that moment she had to make a choice: *get clean or die.*

She stopped using cold turkey, slept for a week, gained 20 pounds, went on to graduate, magna cum laude - and never looked back. Shortly after graduating, she began working as a psychosocial rehabilitation program counselor, later earned her certification, and was promoted to a substance abuse counselor with court-ordered clients.

She was welcomed back into her son's life when he was seven; he is now 17. She has been clean for 10 years, remarried in 2013, and welcomed three more children into her family.

Blu is currently pursuing a Master of Human Services degree in Child Protection.

She credits her son for helping her find recovery and for ultimately saving her life. She also tributes reading about others who were successful, despite having encountered addiction to her recovery since, as she stated, addiction "can have such a stigma and make you feel like you'll never amount to anything."

"Anyone who is going through addiction, I want them to know they can get through this! It can get better if you take the necessary steps," she told me. "You have to want to conquer your own demons. Your story doesn't have to be another tragic tale of a drug overdose. Be the exception. Be the fighter. Be the one who got through it and can look addiction in the eyes and say, 'I beat you!'"

She also had something to tell the loved ones of users.

"There are always underlying issues," she said. "They don't want to be this way. They don't want to lie, cheat, and steal their way through life. They are drowning but have to want sobriety more than you want it for them. I battled addiction and actually won. I took my life back, that's freedom."

Let this story be a reminder that addiction is a chronic disease[80] that does not discriminate. Many still believe addiction only impacts a certain "type" of person. Addiction can and will take any life at any time.

2017 Update:

Blu has one year of schooling remaining until she earns her master's degree. She has been happily married for eleven years. Her oldest son is now 18-years-old.

"I was able to pick myself up, dust myself off, and be the best parent, wife, and version of myself I could be," said Blu. "I'm happy, and my children are as well. I couldn't ask for anything better. Your past does not define you, and you can move past traumatic events and live a happily fulfilled life."

---

[80] https://archives.drugabuse.gov/about/welcome/aboutdrugabuse/chronicdisease/

MEET LARA

"There was never a moment in my young life when I imagined I would become reliant on prescription pills," said Lara, whose experimentation with pills grew into a five-year, full-blown addiction. "I come from the most loving, well-educated, successful, and kind family. I don't recall much trauma in my young life."

Lara, who grew up in an upper-middle-class community, is describing the drug users of today. There was a time when one would be shocked to learn an upstanding citizen was also addicted to drugs; but opiates, ranging from prescription pills to heroin, have infiltrated all areas of the country and all levels of society.[81]

Lara was very well liked but does admit to obsessively seeking validation, especially from her mother, whom she believed loved her sister more. Lara, believing her mother's adoration of her sister stemmed from her sister's intelligence, became focused on getting good grades, extra-curricular activities, and doing whatever she could to make her parents proud.

Her drive to succeed academically continued as she entered college. She received two academic scholarships to Arizona State University and made Dean's List every semester. She graduated Summa Cum Laude in less than four years.

---

[81] http://www.drugrehab.us/news/changing-face-heroin-addiction

"I was far more interested in studying than partying," recounted Lara, whose college was named one of the top ten "party schools" in the United States by Playboy Magazine.[82] "Most of my friends wanted to party, drink, and meet guys. It wasn't my thing. I wanted to stay in my dorm room and write or study. I wanted to do well in school so I could have the grades to be accepted to a good graduate school and obtain my Master's degree in Business Administration (MBA)."

"My sister entered law school during my junior year of college, and it was my goal to enter graduate school as well. I was in constant competition with my sister," added Lara.

Lara graduated from college when she was 21 and underwent minor surgery. She was prescribed opiates.

Though Lara had never previously abused drugs, prescription or otherwise, the timing of her surgery and medication was during a time of immense stress and pressure.

"I was studying for the GMAT, and I knew my entrance to graduate school relied on my score on this test," explained Lara, who would go on to score above average. "The opiates took away the pressure. They calmed me. They allowed me to be at peace."

Opiates initiate the release of dopamine in the brain, creating feelings of pleasure and euphoria. Due to the intense high, opiates are extremely addictive and can cause measurable symptoms of addiction in as little as three days.[83]

---

[82] http://www.phoenixnewtimes.com/news/arizona-state-university-back-in-playboy-party-school-rankings-6640244

[83] http://drugabuse.com/library/the-effects-of-opiate-use

Like all prescriptions, Lara's ran out. Like many pill abusers, she found other ways to get more, from finding an old prescription of hers from a wisdom tooth extraction to stealing prescriptions from her parents, the people she spent the first 21 years of her life trying to impress. Once those prescriptions ran out, Lara stopped taking opiates.

During this time, she was accepted into the graduate program at Pepperdine University.

"I was on the road to success," said Lara. "I had a dream to work in the entertainment industry in a high-level business role, and I was about to make this dream come to life. At Pepperdine, I was respected and well liked. I obtained positions of leadership, and I made friends easily."

Things seemed to be back to "normal" for Lara. However, during the summer after her first-year of graduate school, she discovered tramadol and began to take a pill a day. Tramadol, sold under the brand name Ultram among others, is an opiate.[84]

"This was uncharacteristic of me. So, after a couple of months of doing this, and being unable to stop on my own, I went to a psychiatrist at my grad school," remembered Lara. "I told him I believed that I was addicted to these drugs."

His solution? He prescribed Lara Xanax, Ambien[85], and an anti-depressant.

---

[84] https://www.drugs.com/tramadol.html

[85] https://www.drugs.com/ambien.html

Lara continued to excel at Pepperdine and was offered a full-time, high-level position with the Discovery Channel during her second year at graduate school.

"I graduated at 23-years-old. I was very young to hold an MBA and to be making nearly six figures. I had finally become what I was so longing to be. My parents were incredibly proud of me. My sister would respect me. Things were good. Until they weren't."

Lara worked at the Discovery Channel for three years and began dating a man who had moved from Arizona to California for their relationship and to pursue a law degree.

"He was physically and verbally abusive, but I loved him. I was attracted to him because he was going to be a lawyer," she said. "He started missing Arizona, and I started abusing tramadol again, and he wanted to move back to Arizona. I quit my dream job to please him."

Together and now engaged, they moved back to Arizona, bought a house, and began fighting. At first, it was verbal; then it escalated to a physical altercation where Lara was hurt, and the police were called to their home.

"I felt defeated. I felt like a failure," admitted Lara. "My relationship was over. I had lost my dream job. My home had to be short-sold. Everything was falling apart. My identity was tied to my career, and without a career, I felt like I was nothing."

Lara moved back to California and worked a short-term job in television production. Then, she got into a severe car accident.

"I was prescribed more pills than you could even imagine. Of course, I began abusing them."

A few months later, Lara landed a job as a Vice President of Sales for an entertainment group, putting her back on track for success. Two days before she was supposed to begin, the investors pulled out, and they could not bring her on board.

"I lost the job. I became depressed and suicidal," expressed Lara. "My friends told me to call my psychiatrist and tell him what was going on. I called him, and he said he had the answer for me."

His answer, once again, was prescribing Lara medication, this time Adderall.

"From that moment, I began a long journey into addiction and the darkest time of my life."

Lara chooses not to relay every single detail of what happened during her active addiction. She tells me she lived in her car, stayed in seedy hotels, and hopped in and out of psych wards and rehabs, destroying every important relationship in her life in the process.

"I got sober because I stopped thinking about what I deserved and started thinking about what the world deserved," explained Lara. "I realized how selfish I had become. I didn't recognize myself in the mirror. I was deeply, deeply unhappy."

Lara worked a 12-step program for nearly a year and a half and it helped set her free. However, she believes in the power of holistic recovery and evidence-based treatment, too.

"I received much of this at my last treatment center, and they were able to identify and help fix a problem I had ignored for many years," said Lara. "I was obsessed with men. I had a love addiction during my drug addiction. If I couldn't get high off drugs, I was going to get high off men. I started working with a sex and love addiction therapist, I read countless books on the subject, and I worked some of the steps in the Sex and Love Addiction Anonymous (SLAA) program."[86]

"I threw the book at my recovery. I listened. I did everything that people suggested, and I formed a relationship with God that is indescribable to this day, because of how good it feels to truly know God," added Lara, who grew even more once she discovered Hip Sobriety's eight-week virtual course.[87]

Believing sharing our stories allows others to do the same, Lara started blogging and speaking publicly about her addiction.

"I have become a fierce truth-teller, and I do not deny or hide any part of my story," announced Lara. "I think it is important for women to stand up and share their experiences and tell the world that we don't need drugs and alcohol and that sobriety is one of the best gifts anyone could give themselves."

Lara has become a powerhouse in the recovery community, but her true passion is helping other women recover and feel empowered.

---

[86] https://slaafws.org/

[87] http://www.thehipsobrietyproject.com/

"I plan to form a holistic recovery business that is for women, by women. There are hardly any programs of recovery that are dedicated exclusively to women. The main programs, and even some of the lesser-known programs, were all created by men."

- Alcoholics Anonymous (AA) – *man*
- Narcotics Anonymous (NA) – *man*
- Refuge Recovery[88] – *man*
- Recovery 2.0[89] – *man*
- Smart Recovery[90] – *man*

"I think our treatment of addiction and the story we tell ourselves about recovery is deeply flawed," said Lara. "I do not want to focus on our defects and our powerlessness. I want to focus on our power. I want women to wake up to their lives and see the beauty and awareness and presence that sobriety offers."

No longer searching for anyone's validation, Lara has now dedicated her life to validating and empowering others.

Contact Lara: www.LaraFrazier.com

Listen to Lara:

- www.homepodcast.org/episodes//episode-71-lara-frazier-love-addiction
- www.needyhelper.com/the-alcohol-psychosis-and-why-putting-female-and-male-sex-addicts-in-the-same-treatment-centre-isnt-a-good-idea/

---

[88] http://www.refugerecovery.org/

[89] http://recovery2point0.com/

[90] http://www.smartrecovery.org/

A Variation of this was Originally Published on the Huffington Post on October 10, 2016

MEET MATT AND ADDICTION UNSCRIPTED

As American lawmakers are grappling with ways to respond to what many are calling the worst drug crisis in American history[91], online support communities have taken a stand.

Addiction Unscripted Founder, Matt Mendoza is part of this movement. Since its inception in April of 2015, the website has been visited millions of times.

No, that is not an overstatement. Millions.

Mendoza himself is in recovery and has shared his own personal story of rock bottom and recovery, which included waking up in a holding cell seven years ago at the U.S./Mexico border, while going through the second day of opiate withdrawal and being picked up by the secret service for crimes he had committed to maintain his addiction.

"Two years ago, I thought my life was over," wrote Mendoza in a blog post from 2011, three days after his release from prison.[92] "I remember being driven by the Secret Service from Mexico to an Orange County jail; it was the longest most demoralizing drive of my life."

---

[91] http://www.pbs.org/wgbh/frontline/article/how-bad-is-the-opioid-epidemic/

[92] https://addictionunscripted.com/letters-to-myself-after-leaving-federal-prison-5-years-ago/

"However, I can look back now and point to that day as being the start of what yielded the most joyful and productive two years of my life. As I remind myself of that, I can once again say that today was a good day. I feel blessed," he added."

His mission now is to help others through Addiction Unscripted. The platform is simultaneously a publication and publishing platform and allows anyone to create an account and share their stories, opinions, and articles with the far-reaching community of readers and healers. Topics have included views and experiences on every angle of addiction, brokenness, and recovery.

Addiction Unscripted aims to pull the covers back on the true world of addiction and recovery, relying on the community as a whole to share in the conversation.

The website has teamed up with some of the most talented and influential voices in this field, from all over the world, like Facing Addiction.[93]

"I have long been an advocate for breaking the stigma that addiction is a 'moral failing.' It's this dangerous way of thinking that has kept so many people affected by addiction from seeking the treatment they need," said Mendoza. "I thought about just how powerful technology has been for other social movements by giving rise to a new generation of activism."

In the early stages of Addiction Unscripted, Mendoza partnered with Jason Smith[94], who played a major part in the foundation of the Company.

---

[93] https://www.facingaddiction.org/

[94] https://addictionunscripted.com/author/caliwop88gmail.com/

"I became increasingly motivated to create something after really connecting to a story I had read about the recovery of a writer named Jason Smith. His story was so similar to mine, and I felt like I had known him before I even reached out to him," recalled Mendoza. "There's something special that happens when you hear your own story within someone else's. When I reached out to Jason, I noticed that he was looking for a new job, and I pitched him my idea for a community that could centralize the ideas, thoughts, and stories of those in recovery."

The site has been successful at giving a voice to the often stigmatized and voiceless, allowing them to reveal their stories to those who need to hear them, and provide hope that can only come from unity in struggle.

With about 120 deaths per day due to overdose[95], Mendoza believes Addiction Unscripted has the best resources for family members of those who are struggling with addiction.

Additionally, those battling addiction and/or who are in recovery, have a place where they can share with others who know exactly what it is like to struggle with this disease, including Mendoza.

Those with Substance Use Disorder often feel shame, guilt, and isolation, and detach from the "real world" in response. Addiction Unscripted aims to prove that no one is truly alone by sharing experiences, starting discussions, and by allowing readers to comment on one another's stories.

---

[95] https://www.rt.com/usa/311023-congress-heroin-epidemic-source/

Drug-related deaths now outnumber deaths from gunshot wounds (over 33,600) and motor vehicle crashes (over 32,700) in the United States, according to the CDC.[96]

The collateral damage of these tragedies need a safe haven and Addiction Unscripted is just that, for many.

2017 Update:

The Addiction Unscripted website has over gone a complete design and development change. New features include in-frame video submissions and a new podcast hosted by Claire Rudy Foster.[97]

The podcast follows the format of the two pilot episodes that were released last spring, which is a narrative-style podcast, the only one that exists in the addiction/recovery field.[98]

The website also has added a valuable resource for those looking for treatment, which includes the "Treatment Center Directory."

"We've taken the same idea from allowing users to create their own blogs on our site, and we've done the same thing for treatment centers," explained Mendoza.

---

[96] http://www.cnsnews.com/news/article/susan-jones/dea-drug-overdoses-kill-more-americans-car-crashes-or-firearms

[97] http://www.portlandmercury.com/books/2016/10/19/18640571/claire-rudy-fosters-literature-of-addiction

[98] https://soundcloud.com/addiction-unscripted

The new directory is populated with 14,000 treatment centers in the U.S., and the rehabs themselves can claim their listing page and add their own content to it, including pictures and videos.

"In addition, we have implemented a feature that allows for anyone to rate their experience with that treatment center, so that people can use other people's experience to help choose the right facility," added Mendoza. "It will help take some of the guess work out of such an important decision, especially in an industry in which it's so hard to decipher the good and bad actors."

Another recent addition to Addiction Unscripted is its new Facebook group called *Affected by Addiction Support.*

"It's a closed group, which is comforting to people so that they can share about their own experience with addiction, or that of a loved one, without having the rest of Facebook being able to see their posts," said Mendoza.

The group was just started in December of 2016, and in one month became the largest private group on the topic of addiction and recovery.

To date, there are over 18,000 members. Join the movement here: *facebook.com/groups/AddictionUnscriptedSupport.*

Addiction Unscripted has also been recognized by sources such as the LA Times, The Guardian, Huffington Post, and a plethora of other media publications.

MEET COURTNEY

"I never thought I would be one of the few lucky ones to make it out alive," said Courtney, who has asked to use her middle name.

In a world where up to 90% of heroin users in recovery relapse, Courtney has maintained her sobriety since November 25, 2013.[99]

"I came from a wonderful, religious family. My parents never drank, they never even fought," Courtney told me. "We went to church every time the doors were open. I had the most support and love any girl could ever ask for; but something was missing, I felt so alone for some reason."

Courtney started experimenting with drinking and marijuana at age 15. That was only the beginning. Throughout high school, she would continue to experiment with harder drugs and drink nearly every day, be it with friends or alone in her room.

She graduated high school but quickly failed out of college due to her drug use.

When she was 19, she was introduced to OxyContin.[100]

---

[99] http://healthresearchfunding.org/shocking-heroin-relapse-statistics/

[100] https://www.drugs.com/oxycontin.html

"The feeling that took over my body after I had snorted that pill was a one I never wanted to lose," admitted Courtney. "I did everything I had to do to make sure I didn't go without that feeling for long."

Courtney betrayed everyone she loved, lying and stealing from them, pawning their prized possessions.

She lost the people who mattered the most to her because they no long mattered the most to her; her next high was the only thing that mattered.

"I lost my friends, and my family cut me off. I lost my relationship with God," recounted Courtney. "I lost any dreams or aspirations I had for my life. I let myself go physically, mentally, and emotionally. I was a whole new kind of lost."

Her father would beg her to stop, warning her that if she didn't, she was going to end up dead or in jail, but Courtney didn't listen. She just continued on the self-destructive path addiction had placed her.

Fellow drug users she knew began driving down to Florida to attain pills at pain clinics, and Courtney followed suit.

"I thought it was cool. A few day trips would have me high for weeks," explained Courtney. "It seemed totally worth it to me, until it wasn't. Until making the decision to get high, stay up all night, and drive down there changed my life in about two minutes flat."

Those two minutes wouldn't just change Courtney's life, but the lives of many others, both directly and indirectly.

Courtney, along with two other girls, got into a terrible car accident on the interstate. The accident took the driver's life and landed Courtney and the other passenger in the hospital.

"I was admitted with a head injury, two broken legs and arms, a ruptured spleen, appendix, and gallbladder, among many other injuries," said Courtney, who was placed on a ventilator during this time. "I was in the hospital for months and then went back to my parents' house in a wheelchair. I had to see a physical therapist and basically learn how to walk all over again."

"Something like that would change a lot of people's lives for the better, and I wanted to get clean more than anyone will ever know. I was tired of living the way I was living," added Courtney.

However, that is not what happened. Courtney, addicted to pills, began receiving her pain pills legally, through prescriptions. She abused them; the prescriptions dried up, and Courtney once again spiraled out of control.

"I shoplifted, stole from people I loved, landed in jail five times, got kicked out of rehab for getting high...," Courtney listed, trailing off. "I finally got court ordered to a long term treatment center where I stayed for 16 months and then moved out."

At this point, Courtney was able to maintain sobriety for 25 months. Then her grandfather, best friend, and aunt all passed away within a short span of time.

To numb herself, Courtney relapsed, and this time, she graduated to heroin.

"The heroin took over more than any drug I had ever done," said Courtney. "I went through $40,000 of my insurance money from the car wreck. I went down a rabbit hole I never thought I would emerge alive from."

Courtney fell ill due to her drug use and was told by her doctor she would need a liver transplant by the time she was 24 if she didn't get clean. After a weeklong stay in the hospital due to liver problems, Courtney discovered she was pregnant.

"I knew things had to change; my baby didn't deserve that."

While on probation, Courtney detoxed, distanced herself from triggers like certain people and places, got clean, and gave birth to her son, who was born free of drugs and not addicted.

That was over 37 months ago, and she has not used since the day she discovered she was pregnant.

"I don't weigh 90 pounds soaking wet anymore, and my face isn't hollow. I feed myself. I see a doctor when I'm sick, I sleep eight hours a night, I have a job I've held down for years now, I'm in college finishing my degree, and my most important role in life is that I'm a mother," said Courtney.

"My son saved my life. My hero is a little two-and-a-half-year-old boy with an infectious laugh and a heart of gold. My goal in life is to give him the best life possible because he saved mine."

Courtney completed her probation and will be having the felonies on her record expunged this year. She has found God again. Her life is better than she could have ever imagined.

"I never thought sobriety would be possible," expressed Courtney. "I never thought I would live to see my 30th birthday, but that's coming up. I'm so incredibly grateful."

Courtney's story is important because people need to be constantly reminded that recovery is possible. We need to remember that there is still hope in addiction, regardless of the polarizing statistics. Listening to the stories of success and triumphs of others can help others find hope and motivation, too.

Courtney will celebrate her birthday in March.

"Addiction doesn't know any boundaries
of age, race, ethnicity, or gender.
We need to tackle this
by every means possible."

Tom MacArthur
Here's the Story: A Family Disease.

AFTERWORD

Written By: Congressman Tom MacArthur
macarthur.house.gov

A few years ago, I lost a close friend to addiction. He was passionate, hardworking, and a dedicated family man. He didn't look "like an addict," but his family now lives with the terrible aftermath of their loss. This was a major wake-up call for my family and me.

Losing someone changes your perspective on life, and I know the same is true for Alicia Cook. I had the pleasure of working with Alicia when she approached me to participate in the documentary, *Here's the Story: A Family Disease*, about her cousin, Jessica.

Alicia is engaging communities in a brand new, innovative way. The face of addiction is changing rapidly, and Alicia is at the forefront of the movement to raise awareness about the challenges those battling addiction and their families face. We need more people like Alicia fighting for our communities.

It is time to change the way we address addiction in today's world. Yes, you can make it through this and recover. Yes, we are here for you and your family members. It is time to come together as a community and a nation to address this epidemic head-on.

I know Alicia is doing her part to join our community members in this fight - let's make sure she isn't doing it alone. As co-chair of the House Bipartisan Heroin Task Force, I stand with Alicia in her fight for prevention, treatment, and recovery.

THE DOCUMENTARY

The Emmy-nominated documentary series, *Here's the Story*, kicked off a new season in the fall of 2016 with an episode entitled, "A Family Disease."

Produced by Steve Rogers, the documentary followed writer Alicia Cook, who lost her cousin Jessica to a heroin overdose. The 29-minute documentary was filmed over the course of six months and watches as Cook, her family, and fellow advocates discuss openly how the disease of addiction alters not only the life of the user, but the entire family, forever.

Here's the Story: A Family Disease
is available online:

www.njtvonline.org/programs/driving-jersey/heres-the-story-a-family-disease

63816142R00097

Made in the USA
Lexington, KY
18 May 2017